# Tips for Women at Work

# Tips for Women at Work

*Kickstart your career*

### Edited by Anna M. Maslin
PhD, MSc, BA (Hons), RGN

International Officer for Nursing & Midwifery,
The Department of Health, England

Professor, School of Health, Community and Education Studies
Northumbria University, UK

Chair, Commonwealth Health Ministers Steering Committee
for Nursing and Midwifery

Published by Northumbria University
Trinity Building, Newcastle upon Tyne NE1 8ST, UK

First Published 2003

Copyright © Anna M. Maslin unless otherwise stated.

All rights reserved. No part of this publication may be reproduced or transmitted in any form or by any means, electronic or mechanical, including photocopy, recording, or any information storage and retrieval system, without permission in writing from the publisher. This book is sold subject to the condition that it shall not, by way of trade or otherwise, be lent, re-sold, hired out or otherwise circulated without the publishers prior consent.

British Library Cataloguing in Publication Data. A Catalogue Record for this book is available from the British Library.

ISBN 186135 292 1

Designed and printed by the Department of External Relations, Northumbria University

Northumbria University is the trading name of the University of Northumbria at Newcastle.
ER-61241

*FOR
Sarah
Alex
Charlotte
and
Victoria*

## With many thanks to

Stephen and Mabel
as always

## Also special thanks to the following for their words of support and all their kindness

To all the contributors and

Sarah Mullally

Professor Tony Dickson

Andy Peden Smith

Andrew G. White

Professor Trevor Powles

Kyle, Ryan and Antonia

# CONTENTS

**FOREWORD**
Sarah Doukas — ix

**INTRODUCTION**
Anna M. Maslin — xiii

**CHAPTER 1**
*Preparing Yourself*
Anna M. Maslin — 1

**CHAPTER 2**
*Cracking the CV*
Tom Storrow — 7

**CHAPTER 3**
*Interview Intelligence*
Tom Storrow — 23

**CHAPTER 4**
*Salaries and Individual Performance Reviews*
Jennifer Parr — 37

**CHAPTER 5**
*Personal Presentation*
April Brown — 55

**CHAPTER 6**
    *Managing Home, Work and Time*
        Andrée le May      63

**CHAPTER 7**
    *What about the Kids?*
        Sue Harrop and Sue Miller      71

**CHAPTER 8**
    *Dealing with the Unexpected, Stress and Bullies*
        Catherine Gaskell      91

**CHAPTER 9**
    *Work-Life Balance, Flexi-time and Working from Home*
        Anna M. Maslin      111

**CHAPTER 10**
    *A Personal View...*
        Heather Angel      117
        Dame Lorna Muirhead      124
        Rosie Barnes      129
        Linda Conlon      133

**CHAPTER 11**
    *Conclusion*
        Anna M. Maslin      137

**Contributors' Profiles**      141

*The views expressed in this book are those of the authors and are not a statement of Government Policy.*

# FOREWORD

## Sarah Doukas

I first met Anna a few years ago when she approached me for an interview and contribution for her successful book *Women at Work*. I thought it was an invaluable tool for today's working woman, and I was delighted to be asked to write the foreword for her follow-up book *Tips for Women at Work*. I have been a working woman since I was seventeen, and have a wealth of experience gained from many years in business, but Anna's book provides practical and informed advice to make achieving success in the workplace easier.

It's not easy being a woman in today's workplace. Women's roles have changed dramatically over the decades and today's modern woman has been programmed to believe that she should be a high achiever professionally, an amazing partner and a perfect mother. Anything less is viewed as an under-achievement of sorts. Personally, I think all women should set their own agendas and recognise and applaud their own levels of success. Whether they be in the boardroom or the playroom.

I have been the Managing Director of the Storm Model Agency for the past 15 years. However, I never set out to become a model agent – along the way I ran an antiques business at Clignancourt Market in Paris and managed a punk band in London during the mad mid-1970s. I have always known that I wanted to be my own boss and work for myself and I left school before sitting my A Level's. Up until that point I had been privately educated – but I then rebelled against my academic father, who had dreams of university and a more traditional and professional career for me, and I set off on an amazing adventure.

I actually modelled for a while, moved to Paris, married my first husband – a musician, and then lived in San Francisco for a few years where I gave birth to my first child. When I finally returned to the UK in 1980 I had a young daughter in private education to support and bills to pay. I managed to talk my way into a job with a top modelling agency. Although I didn't have any fashion experience,

I had learnt a lot managing the band, and I was organised, efficient and confident – all valuable qualities.

I started at the bottom of the ladder, making tea and trips to the dry cleaners for my boss. The hours were long, the atmosphere stressful, and there were frequently problems with model bookings. At the beginning the majority of my salary went on paying my childcare costs. Though I was commuting across London on public transport with my daughter in tow, I had finally found a profession I loved, and I was determined to learn as much as I could. After a few years I had worked my way to the top and was running the agency, and after 7 years I was ready for new challenges. I left to pursue my dream.

I was bursting with ideas and put them into a detailed and comprehensive business plan. I foresaw a gap in the market, a need for UK-based models to be represented and marketed from the UK, to clients all around the world. I had established a valuable network of agents in various influential markets that I still work with closely, and I wanted to open up the UK market to more lucrative and creative opportunities. I wanted to establish the first international model agency that operated from the UK.

I have always been very proactive about achieving my ambitions and realistic about my professional strengths and weaknesses. I have a talent for recognising and realising the potential in people, whether staff or models. I'm also good at spotting talent, 'new faces' that may be interesting, edgy, beautiful but ultimately photogenic. I'm a great motivator, organiser and multi-tasker and I'm calm under fire too. My financial experience then, was limited, and knowing I needed some expert help, I enlisted the services of a really good lawyer and a fantastic accountant who both decided to support me in my efforts to find financial backing for my fledgling company. They warned me it would be difficult to find backing, but they liked my drive and determination and my fresh ideas for the business.

I met with several 'city types' to discuss finance and partnerships. These included Adam Faith and Miles Copeland who had managed the band *The Police* and several financial controllers and bankers who had little or no understanding of fashion or the modelling business. There was lots of offers but none of the interested parties felt right and I didn't want to sign a deal with the wrong partner.

Ironically, I never once thought about failure, and this ultimately kept me focused and strong. At the eleventh hour I signed a deal with Richard Branson whose sister I had gone to school with. He was happy to accept the terms I offered and backed me through his private company, Voyager. We signed a deal that allowed us both to be equal partners. I would be given autonomous control and support from Richard if I needed it. These conditions provided the opportunity for Storm to flourish and I managed to repay Richard his start-up loan within the first 3 years of the company trading.

Today I employ thirty staff and run the agency with my brother Simon, who came on board in the early days. I was travelling with Simon in 1988 when I spotted Kate Moss at JFK airport in New York. She was fourteen, 5'6" tall and had a different look to any of the 'supermodels' that were gracing the pages of all the glossies at the time. I didn't care, Kate had something about her, an attitude, an individuality, a look and I thought she was great. I couldn't have predicted then how famous or successful she would become but I still represent her today, nearly 15 years later.

I now have three children whose ages are five, eleven and twenty-three, and the company has expanded quite organically to include a Men's Division, a New Faces Division and a theatrical agency – Storm Artists' Management. I also have two model agencies in South Africa, one in Johannesburg and another in Cape Town that specialises in Sports Management and Production.

Life can be stressful and I am incredibly busy, but I surround myself with a good team of predominantly female staff who provide a solid support network, and they allow me to get on with the business of running and developing the company. It's important that everyone works well together and gets on with the models, and I make great efforts to get the chemistry right at Storm. Whilst I also employ male staff and I think mine are incredible, I find that more women in general have the necessary qualities to be good bookers. Women are born organisers, very intuitive and able to spot potential problems, calm under stress and naturally emphatic when it comes to dealing with people. I also look for strong characters who can 'nurture' the young inexperienced models but also 'manage' the more recognisable 'supermodels' we represent.

Today, I'm still as motivated and enamoured of the business and the models I represent as I was 15 years ago. If I was asked to offer advice to women in employment, or looking for employment, it would be to find a career you like, work hard, and don't be afraid of getting down to the business of making your plans a reality.

# Introduction

**Anna M. Maslin**

*Tips for Women at Work* comes as a follow-up to *Women at Work* (2002). *Women at Work* recognised the huge interest in the role of women at work globally. It acknowledged that many governmental and non-governmental organisations are hoping to increase the number of women in key positions and that the British government is committed to sexual equality, to family friendly working policies, to flexible working and support for the working mother. *Women at Work* aimed to learn from the experiences of a group of outstanding women who have faced huge challenges and achieved outstanding results. Women in all walks of life perform daily miracles, in the care and work they provide for their families, society and the economy. We all acknowledge it is wise to learn from the mistakes and experiences of others. *Women at Work* in a unique way allowed us to glimpse into the lives of an exceptional cohort. *Women at Work* also acknowledged that success and value do not necessarily equate with salary and status, understanding that success will mean different things to different people.

*Women at Work* is a combination of substantive chapters dealing with the relevant issues for women in, or hoping to be in, challenging personal roles and has contributions from women who have achieved excellence in their own unique worlds. This is combined with chapters which aim to explore; the theory and practicality of the dilemmas surrounding the desire for success, however that is defined, who these 'successful' women are, what drives them to succeed, what qualities or coping mechanisms do they have to achieve success and finally is success worth it?

*Tips for Women at Work* moves on a stage. *Tips for Women at Work* is a practical resource focusing on areas that many women find a challenge. How do we actually get moving and start progressing towards the kind of work we would really enjoy? How do we crack the all-important CV? How should we present ourselves at interview? What are the skills and techniques involved? How do we address the salary issue? No-one needs me to tell them that women generally speaking are not earning the same as men. Women sometimes lack the knowledge, skills and expertise in salary negotiation. What about personal presentation? Sometimes we are concentrating so hard on getting the qualifications or getting the job done that we don't realise the visual impact we make on people by not giving this aspect a little more thought. What about time management? Women are brilliant at multi-tasking but again sometimes there are principles and tricks we can learn to help us manage our day-to-day lives. What about the kids? For most women this is one of the biggest areas of concern. If we are working because we need to provide financially for our children and giving up work is not an option how do we ensure our children's health and happiness and our own sanity? What about stress and bullies? Sadly there are occasions often more frequently than we would choose when we are forced to deal with these unpleasant situations. How should we respond so we are not victims? Finally work-life balance – how can we achieve a balance and a style of working which is productive and sane?

There are many books on the market which deal with aspects of these subjects, many of which are excellent, but this book is different because it focuses on a unique combination of areas that many women feel are vitally important and addresses these issues from a woman's perspective.

I hope this book will be of interest to all women, but especially those women who are considering a life change or those who want to gain insight from the knowledge and experience of others. *Tips for Women at Work* is a book which aims to increase awareness of the issues facing successful women, to increase understanding, to provide inspiration and to encourage women to achieve their own unique brand of success. I know I have learnt a great deal and enjoyed reading all the contributions. I hope you will too.

# Chapter 1
## *Preparing Yourself*

**Anna M. Maslin**

### Introduction

Well you decided now is the time! Time to make a move at work, time to go back to work or time to start looking for work. The thought of taking such a big step can leave you with a queasy feeling in the pit of your stomach not to mention a number of sleepless nights. Life changes no matter how big or small can range from making you feel really excited to stressed beyond belief.

We may be making a change for a number of reasons. We may need to earn more money to support our children. We may need to give our brains a much-needed kickstart. We may want to use our talents for the benefit of mankind.

When preparing yourself you need to focus on a number of issues. This book concentrates on a number of key areas many working women will find useful to have thought through. These will include applications, CV, interview techniques, salaries, Individual Performance Review, personal presentation, managing home, work and time, issues with childcare, dealing with the unexpected, stress, bullies and even a little on flexi-working and working from home.

Whilst I fully support the fact that education is one of the key factors in enabling a person to have the tools to succeed I am assuming that the majority of people reading this book are at a point in their lives where they want to find a satisfying job with the qualifications, skills and expertise they already possess. In some cases a woman will be in a position to undertake a degree or professional qualification which will involve the investment of substantial time and money but for many it may not be possible at this time. Even if you do not have a vast formal education you can optimise the skills you have on offer to make yourself as attractive as possible to a future employer.

One of the key ways you can prepare yourself is to take the time to quietly consider a few questions. Buy yourself a small notepad and have a quick brainstorm.

- What formal qualifications do I already possess?
- What informal qualifications do I have?
- Do I have any particular skills or talents?
- What do I enjoy spending my time on?
- Would I prefer to work with my head or my hands? Or both?
- Will my health stand up to my choice of work?
- Will I be on my feet for long periods?
- Will I be putting a strain on my back?
- Will I be putting myself under a great deal of stress for little reward?
- What would my ideal career be?
- What have I enjoyed in jobs undertaken so far?
- Do I want to take a job which will allow me time, and or money, to facilitate me in being able to gain additional qualifications for a career, which will be my longer-term goal?
- What is available locally?
- Am I prepared to travel?
- Is childcare or other responsibilities going to impact on my choice of work?
- Is my partner or family supportive?
- If I died tomorrow what would I wish I had spent my time on?

## What resources are available locally to help me gain information or additional skills?

- Where is the library?
- Where is my local job centre?
- Is there an Internet facility available locally?
- Can someone show me how to use the Internet?
- Is there someone locally who can provide me with vocational advice?
- Are there free basic PC skills courses available in my area for adult learners?
- Am I eligible for any other free or low cost adult educational opportunities?
- Is there vocational guidance at my current place of employment?
- Do I belong to a union that has a careers advice service?
- Do I belong to a professional organisation that will give free advice?
- Is there a government department who deals with the career I would like to embark on?

## Have I considered working for myself?

- If I would like to be self-employed, do I know how to write a business plan?
- Do I know who to talk to, to get advice?
- Do I know someone trustworthy who is self-employed who will share his or her experiences honestly?
- Do I have the facilities, i.e. premises and equipment to set up a business?
- Do I know a trustworthy accountant?
- Do I have the support of a good bank?

Shirley Conran, back in 1977, observed:

> *'Careers advisory officers all made surprisingly similar comments on mistakes that women make when they want to go back to work.'*

Here are fourteen:

## Mistake 1

'She really made her biggest mistake when she stopped work and assumed that, because she was bringing up children, she would never have a job again.'

## Mistake 2

'She assumed that she'd never want a job again.'

## Mistake 3

'Never assume that because you're interested in children when your own are young that you have a universal interest in children that will last for life. It rarely does... If a mother wants to start a new job working with children I'd advise her to wait. If she plans to teach 4-year-old infants, she should wait until her youngest is at least 8 years old – then see if she still feels the same way about 4-year-olds.'

## Mistake 4

'She isn't practical about her own abilities... She isn't realistic about the opportunities available... She's too romantic.'

## Mistake 5

'The majority of women returnees I see underestimate their competence and abilities. A woman needs to be a bit more confident. She needs to make a conscious effort to be positive: she mustn't cop out by saying she's shy or hasn't any self-confidence. The family attitude can make or break a woman in this frame of mind: a condescending or tolerantly amused attitude can be crushing.'

## Mistake 6

'The Queen of the Hearth syndrome... The woman who thinks that running a home for a few years automatically equips her to take on anything without training or experience.'

### Mistake 7

Again indicative of a Queen of the Hearth. 'She thinks she's always right... Nobody is allowed to contradict her... She won't fit into other peoples established work pattern and wants to do everything her own way... This is the hardest thing to get a woman to realise about herself. But you've got to see how the system works before laying down the law to other people.'

### Mistake 8

Especially when there are teenagers in the office – and there generally are: 'If you treat teenagers as children (because they're not much older than your own) then you're in for trouble.'

### Mistake 9

'She's so used to being on her own and not working to a set routine that she finds it hard to accept a timetable and stick to it.'

### Mistake 10

'When a woman starts work again she tends to underestimate how much time it takes to run her home in the way she's been doing it. It's often a good idea to have a dummy run a week or two before you start the job.'

### Mistake 11

'Perhaps the saddest mistake that a woman can make is not giving herself the best chance, taking the first job she's offered, not finding out what is available or what she's suited for and never taking advantage of the good free help that's offered in career guidance and training. Over half the women I see don't know what they're good at and don't really know what they want.'

### Mistake 12

Is made when she goes after the job. 'Few women know how important it is to present themselves properly when being interviewed for a job or think in terms of the employer's reason for their meeting. She can be her own worst enemy if she goes on about wanting to take time off to take the children to the dentist: what an employer is least interested in is when you're not going to be there. Wait until you have the job and have proved how valuable you are, then people are generally prepared to make concessions, within reason.'

**Mistake 13**

> Not doing anything (and whining on about it) because there is no immediate opportunity that is exactly right. This often indicates lack of guts, fear of competition, fear of the world outside… and fear of being turned down by some of the people some of the time. Everyone who succeeds has risked failure.'

**Mistake 14**

> 'Giving up to easily.'

Although Shirley Conran wrote this 25 years ago the principles remain largely the same. Although the comments are a little dated in part there is a basic truth, which remains applicable even today.

# Chapter 2
## *Cracking the CV*

**Tom Storrow**

### Introduction

The Curriculum Vitae or CV seems to generate a surprising amount of concern and mystique. Its sole purpose is to get you onto a 'longlist' (the preliminary selection of candidates for further assessment and discussion) or a 'shortlist' (the final selection of candidates for formal interview and/or other assessment) for a particular job[1]. Entry to one of these lists gives you an opportunity to sell yourself and your skills and attributes and to find out more about the employer and the post. Thus, the CV has something of a 'key to the door' nature and so it is important to get it right to enable you to progress towards the job you want.

However, the bookshelves of the management and personal development sections of my local bookstore seem to have plenty of volumes on how to write this fabled 'perfect' CV, so why bother writing a chapter on CVs for this book, apart from the fact that we wish to provide you with a range of practical tips all under one cover?

Well, I happen to believe that a CV is a personal statement. As such, it should reflect the style and personality of the candidate as well as describing their suitability for the specific post for which they are applying. For this reason, I will not attempt here to set out the 'perfect' CV, as this will be quite different for different individuals and especially for different posts. I believe that the idea that there is a perfect standard CV, regardless of the individual, the post and even the industry, is for charlatans and the gullible.

Let me illustrate my point.

My own background is in the public sector, especially the National Health Service. In the NHS, for senior professional posts and for almost any post above supervisory level, employing bodies will tend to do the following:

- Advertise the post openly in vacancy bulletins and probably in the national, local or professional press inviting potential applicants to send for an Information Pack.

- In the Information Pack provide a Job Description/Role Specification and a Person Specification, plus information about the department or organisation and often background information about the location/schools/house prices, etc.

- Shortlist candidates against the criteria set out in the Specifications.

- Interview candidates before a panel, possibly also asking them to make a presentation, undergo psychometric assessments, etc.

- Take up references and often make informal enquiries (although the validity and fairness of this may be very questionable) about the candidates.

Other, non-public sector, industries often rely upon very different approaches. The following being a reasonable example of such an approach:

- Advertise the post, asking potential candidates to send in their résumé, or for senior posts use recruitment consultants to search out candidates and obtain their résumés.

- Review the résumés received, longlisting those candidates felt to be worthy of more detailed contact.

- Begin an interview/meeting process, during which more information is given to candidates about the organisation and more information is sought from the candidates about themselves (again this may involve panel interviews, psychometric assessments, presentations, etc. at the later stages).

There can be further, very different approaches. My own experience in joining the company for which I work now involved neither CV nor résumé – the company Chairman knew me well, sounded me out about joining them over a glass of beer and made me 'an offer I couldn't refuse' a few days later!

Conversely, I have a number of friends and colleagues who made their first contact with their current employers by sending in a CV 'cold' and asking whether there were any suitable vacancies, rather than responding to an advertisement.

Obviously, there are numerous variations upon and permutations of the themes I have outlined very briefly on the previous page, but the simple point that I wish to make is that different industries and different employers will require and expect different responses and thus different CVs from potential employees. Thus, the only 'perfect' CV can be the one geared perfectly towards a given post with a given employer in a given industry at a given time.

Having said that, I think that there are some principles and some alternatives that are worth considering, and some questions that you can ask yourself in preparing your own perfect, customised CV. I have based the principles and suggestions that follow upon my own research and reading and especially upon the recruitment and personal development experiences that I have had and seen in the NHS and other industries. These are set out below, not in any order of priority and certainly not to be followed slavishly, but rather as points for consideration, reflection and even challenge, which I hope you will find helpful before you complete your own CV.

**Information Packs, phone calls and advance visits**

In most parts of the public sector – and in some other sectors – there is a custom of providing Information Packs to respondents to the job advertisement, and often visits or telephone contacts are offered and indeed encouraged for senior posts. This is not done out of politeness, but usually because public sector employers in particular are bound by rules of equality of opportunity and openness, as well as the normal equality legislation. Thus, they want to ensure that prospective candidates fully understand the requirements of both the post and the organisation and respond to these in their application. Further, this approach can help to 'sell' a post or organisation when there are real recruitment shortages. Additionally, of course, it can also provide some initial contact and thus 'first impressions' of candidates.

(As I indicated above, this is not the case in all industries, and many use the process of asking for a résumé in order to get a quick overview of potential candidates before deciding on a longlist who will be contacted for more detailed discussions, interviews and assessments. There is more on this 'résumé' style of CV to come.)

Therefore, if you are already in the public sector and want a change or promotion – or if you want to get into the public sector – do not just send in a standard résumé, having failed to make contact or obtain the Information Pack. That would be almost a guarantee that you won't even make the first-cut of shortlisting. Indeed in our public sector orientated Recruitment Division, we would not bother looking at the CV of someone who had not sent for the Information Pack, as such a person would be quite unable to respond to the specifications.

## The 'full CV'

Most public sector and some other employers will expect more than a one or two page résumé. They will expect you to have made contact when the position was offered, and they will expect you to have addressed the key issues in their Information Pack.

These issues are usually reasonably obvious, being summarised in the requirements covered by the Role and Person Specifications. At the very least, they will also expect some reference to their organisation in the CV, even if only on the front or title page! However, some employers ask for a statement of what you can do for them, and failure to answer this will almost certainly consign your CV to the wastepaper bin. Even if they do not ask for it explicitly, consider adding a section anyway on why you want this particular post and what skills and experience you will bring to it.

There is no such thing as a 'right' length for this type of fuller CV. It has to be long enough for you to provide the evidence of the qualifications, experiences and skills that enable you to meet their requirements and to tell them why you are the candidate they need, without being boring or pedantic. Perhaps something in the order of three to five pages would be acceptable, but this always must be a matter of personal judgement, based on the impression you want to create and the employer's requirements. For example, medical CVs can be much longer, because prospective consultant surgeons and physicians need to set out in some detail their training, special interests, research and publications.

Obviously, if they ask for 'no more than three pages', then you fail to follow the instructions at your peril – there's more on dealing with such instructions later. However, an obvious tip is not to forget how much room for manoeuvre you can create on the apparent length of a document by playing with the margins, borders (if you have them), font size and style.

Think about the order in which you present your CV. A fairly standard approach is to use about half of the CV to give personal and contact details, qualifications, membership of professional bodies, names and addresses of referees and an outline of your employment history (with just a couple of lines under the recent posts giving a flavour of what they were, scale of responsibilities, etc.). The remainder can then cover key skills and experiences, based clearly on a response to the requirements of the Role and Person Specifications. In these pages, don't be afraid to use the headings from the employer's Role and Person Specifications. By doing so, you can help them to do the shortlisting, which they will probably appreciate – especially if they have lots of applicants – whilst you are also saying, 'Look, I meet your requirements, don't you dare not shortlist me!'

The main alternative is to give the information about your skills and experiences under the headings of each of your current and previous posts (in reverse chronological order, i.e. starting with current job and working back). Make sure that what you write is about your experiences and achievements, not just a potted version of the job description for each post you have held. Employers want to hear what you achieved in the job, not just a list of the duties you were supposed to perform.

If you follow this latter approach, then remember to 'taper' the list of posts, giving less and less detail of the jobs and the experiences, as you go further back, as employers are usually more interested in what you have been doing in the last 3–5 years than what you did 20 years ago. A good example of this 'tapering' is quite often seen in CVs of senior managers in professions such as nursing. Effective CVs in these cases will often bring together in summary form a series of junior posts from early in the individual's career. This can be done partly to save space (there really is no need for potential Directors of Nursing to list out the full details of every Staff Nurse job they held in the 1970s) but also because the summary statement can have much more impact. For example, completing the career history by saying something such as, 'Between 1975 and 1989 I held clinical posts at Staff Nurse and Ward Manager levels in Medical specialties in hospitals in London', is a clear statement that says 'I've got some real clinical/professional experience and credibility.'

In organising your experiences for the CV, again remember what the employer has told you they are seeking. This may mean that you have to be brave and leave out or heavily edit experiences of which you are very proud, but which unfortunately are not relevant to this post. It may also mean 'talking-up' other experiences which are a little thin, but which are important to this post. However, this does not mean fabricating or grossly exaggerating experiences or skills – there is more on this presently.

Having suggested a split of about 50:50 between personal details, education, career history, etc. and skills, experiences and what you have to offer, do think about the order in which this information is presented in your CV. For example, let's say that your CV will run to four pages. If you put your personal and contact details and career history on page one, followed by a two-page skills and experiences section, finishing with the page of education, memberships, referees, etc. this will mean that employers can get into the 'meat' of your real experience more quickly. It is probably better to do this – especially if you are demonstrating that you meet their specifications clearly – than forcing them to read through all of the personal and background stuff before getting to what they really want to see.

In tailoring your CV to the Role and Person Specifications for the job, remember that you may be able to influence the later interview processes, by leaving 'hooks' upon which questions could be hung. For example, you may tell them what you did in a specific situation, but not how you did it – saving that for later!

## The physical appearance of your CV

When it comes to the physical assembly of a fuller length CV, remember what usually happens to CVs in the Personnel Department or at the Recruitment Consultants – i.e. that they are pulled apart and photocopied if they are to be reviewed by several people or if there is to be an interview panel. Thus, if you have a multi-page CV, do not use those forms of binding that will require your CV literally to be ripped apart for copying – what will the edges of each photocopy sheet look like? Consider instead one of the simple slide-and-clip folders/binders that look good but can easily be taken apart and reassembled.

Similarly, do not use strongly coloured paper, which is likely to show up as dark grey when photocopied. One of the most striking CVs I've ever seen was beautifully set out and printed onto red paper. It was stunning, but it had to be retyped by a junior clerk as it produced a photocopy of black print on a dark grey background! The retyping was not perfect and obviously this had some impact on the CV, but this effort was only made for the candidate because she was excellent; otherwise the CV would have been consigned to the reject pile. I suggest using either standard A4 white or at most a cream coloured paper (as this is pleasant on the eye in original form but will also photocopy well). Also, try to use a good quality paper, rather than the flimsy paper out of the office photocopier!

## The résumé CV

As I indicated earlier, there are some employers who will want the two-page (or even one-page) résumé type of CV, either because they have adopted the recruitment approach of making contact and sharing more information after seeing the CV or because they believe that everything they need to know can be summarised in just two pages. This type of CV has been a standard in the USA for some time, not least, as Max Eggert has observed, because of the strong equality legislation there, which has led to the exclusion of almost all personal information.

This type of CV inevitably will have to be more standardised and perhaps less customised to a particular post. Clearly, you can still edit some of the key skills and experiences within the confines of two pages, to try to match what you know about the post, the employer and/or the industry, but much of the CV will have to be of a fairly standard format and content, in order to keep it short.

The résumé format usually comprises the following:

- A brief 'profile', describing you and your skills and attributes
- Basic personal and educational details
- A brief career history – probably no more than 4–5 lines per recent post
- An outline of key skills, experiences, projects, etc.
- A brief statement of intentions/ambitions/why this post (if appropriate)
- Referees (if appropriate).

It is probably only the fourth and fifth points that you may want to customise a little – remember that usually the purpose of a résumé is to have-it-to-hand quickly to open up a dialogue with potential employers or even to use as an introduction to employers to whom you wish to write and send a CV 'cold'.

## Profiles at the top of your CV or résumé

Here I must confess to a personal prejudice. I rarely read profiles, because I find too many of them difficult to take seriously.

The concept of the profile is particularly linked to the development of the two-page résumé mentioned above, in which there is little space to write about personal style and motivation and so the 'profile' is used. In these circumstances, the profile clearly can be very helpful.

Unfortunately, however, in my experience the profile often appears to become an anonymous jumble of mock-American management-speak. For example, I would suggest to you that there is little point in writing something like, 'A highly-motivated, self-starting, experienced and people-focused senior manager with a particular strength in project and performance management'. Unfortunately, I've seen quite a few like that. There is little point in writing it because no one would ever describe himself or herself as anything much different to this. (Can you really imagine anyone writing the opposite: 'A poorly-motivated, slow, inexperienced sociopath, with particular weaknesses in project and performance management!')

Hence, the profile is too often reduced to platitudes and buzzwords. Personally, I'm more interested in the provision of evidence of real achievements, and would rather give over the limited space to that instead of unsupported self-promotion.

In addition, I have a second prejudice to confess – and this shows my age and my tendency to pedantry! The example I've written above is not written in English, as there is no subject or verb. I have an allergy to such damage to the language. I also have a fear – perhaps irrationally – that it may be easier for people to tell me lies when they write in such an impersonal style that they could be referring to anyone.

However, profiles can be helpful in saying something about style and approach in a succinct way, so perhaps it is best to focus on this, and to try to write it in English. For example, 'I am a very experienced and enthusiastic NHS/HR/Production, etc. senior manager, with a good track record of project and performance management at both Board and local service levels. My personal style is based on developing relationships and trust, and I am particularly motivated by change and strategic management issues.'

Having shared some of my prejudices with you, I should remind you that some of these observations and suggestions are highly personal and you might agree with me and want to use some of them or you may violently disagree. That's fine; as I said at the outset, a CV is a personal document and must reflect you, not me or some other writer.

### Use of the first person

My comments above also raise the issue of the use of the first person singular (I, me, etc.) in profiles or in the main body of the CV. Some people say that you should describe yourself in the third person (he, she) or anonymously (a highly motivated manager, etc.), so as to avoid starting every sentence with 'I' and thus running the risk of appearing self-centred.

I would certainly agree that you should not start every line of a bullet-point list of posts held or achievements with 'I did...', 'I held...', etc. However, in a body of text, my own preference is always to write in English, using the first person, but using the great and wonderful variety of the English language to help avoid repetition. For example: 'I worked at... In my particular experience there was... The leadership of the project was offered to me... We delivered...', etc. In some circumstances, the use of the first person plural (we, our) can also be very powerful as an indicator of personal style, if the employer is seeking a team player and leader. However, remember that its overuse might give an impression that others led and you were only a part of a project. To get a balance, I like phrases such as, 'I led XYZ and we achieved...'

### Honesty is the best policy

I mentioned previously the need to edit your skills and experiences to the job requirements. Leaving things out or playing them down if they are not very relevant is fairly easy and straightforward, if sometimes painful. A little more difficult is the issue of 'talking things up'.

It is one thing to make the most of a particular skill or experience and to talk and write quite a lot about something that perhaps you have only done once or twice. However, it quite something else to claim to have qualifications, skills or experiences that you do not have. You might think that this is 'fair game' if you can get away with it, but I suggest that it is not only dishonest but also foolish, often leading to unhappy appointments, based on either deceit or an inability to do the job properly. Further, if you do this and you are found out, it may well be that you will have given your employer grounds to dismiss you. Even if you are not found out directly, you run the risk of it becoming clear in due course that you cannot actually do the job. This is likely to create stress for you if you try to hide it; or a different type of stress if your managers can see it and feel the need to take action!

I can understand people sometimes being desperate to get a job and perhaps feeling prepared to take a risk. However, if you are not in a genuinely life-or-death situation, then why run the risk of losing your job/career or putting yourself under stress for the sake of a pay rise or a grander title?

Further, I always recommend to my personal development clients that they should be themselves throughout a recruitment process. If they do this and the employer likes what they see, then that is great, potentially leading to a perfect match between the person, the post and the organisation. If they do this and the employer does not like what they see, then I would suggest that this is also great – who really wants to be a round peg in a square hole, placed there because they pretended to be a square peg?

**Personal details**

There is some debate about whether or not to include personal interests, hobbies, and other commitments. Some people say that you are applying only for a job and that there is no necessity for this to be linked to your personal life. Others say that employers like to know something about the 'whole person' – particularly as senior and executive-level jobs can be so all-consuming that they inevitably impinge on your personal life anyway; and many jobs today require a degree of mobility and flexibility that our parents would have thought ridiculous.

My view is that unless you feel very strongly, or you know that this employer would frown upon it, why not err on the side of putting in something brief about you as a person, your interests, etc. Remember that it is possible to use this to your advantage, by demonstrating that you can combine a successful career with other aspects of your life, and/or that you are respected in other walks of life, being a school governor, trustee of a charity, honorary lecturer, or whatever. However, if you think that mentioning your personal circumstances as a female will cause problems with a particular employer, then perhaps you need to ask yourself whether you really want to work for them.

There is also some debate about whether to include your age or birth date. I know that some employers might be seen as 'age-ist', but if they shortlist you then they will be able to estimate your age when you meet them, so omitting your age from the CV is only delaying them finding out your likely age. Further, my experience is that when candidates exclude their age or birth date, employers and recruitment specialists are usually curious and so always try to calculate the age from the dates of qualifications, degrees, etc. Thus, my feeling is that it is usually pointless excluding your age.

A different matter is whether to mention family commitments. Unfortunately, some employers will be wary of women with a young family, assuming that they will take more time off. Others might have realised that they need to be flexible and supportive in order to fill their vacancies and so will offer part-time work, flexible contracts or crèche facilities. If the employer appears to be in the latter camp, then you can probably mention children or other commitments in your CV or at interview, if you wish to do so. If they appear to be in the former camp, then I'd probably leave out such personal details.

## Preparing the raw material

If you are in the type of industry that requires the résumé approach to CVs, it is fairly easy to keep your CV up-to-date and ready to use. You should decide upon a format with which you are comfortable and prepare a slightly longer version than the classic two pages – perhaps having a long list of skills and experiences that you can edit down quickly for a particular post or employer. This basic 'raw material' résumé can be reviewed every few months, so that you can add in to the long list new experiences, qualifications, etc.

It is a little more difficult if you will have to prepare a more thoroughly customised and extensive CV, but the same principle applies. Keep your standard two pages of personal details, qualifications and career history as up-to-date as possible. For the rest of the fuller CV, I recommend keeping a paragraph or two on each of your key skills and experiences, and updating and adding to these every few months – this might run to several pages, but don't worry about it; this is your 'catalogue' of CV material, from which you will choose the best items as you need them. It is surprising how quickly we can all forget a really interesting or important experience, when our jobs require us quickly to move on to a new project, target or assignment, so keeping these notes is really helpful. It is then much easier to read through all of these paragraphs and edit them down to fit a particular Role and Person Specification, than to start with a blank sheet of paper.

## Do what they ask and make yourself easy to deal with

I mentioned earlier the use of the employer's own headings and specifications – playing their own words back to them, which they may find flattering, and organising your CV to fit with the specification or schedule against which they are selecting candidates. My colleagues in our Recruitment Division rejoice when a candidate follows the headings given to them, as it makes the assessment of that CV much easier. Think about it for yourself – you set out a specification of your requirements and instructions about how to respond, then you get 100 responses to plough through. Many of them have not followed your instructions, but some of them have; towards which candidates will you be most sympathetic?

Sometimes, employers ask for unusual things. I remember once applying for a senior post in the NHS where the organisation asked in the Information Pack for candidates to apply in the form of a letter to the Chair covering the five key headings of the Person Specification, with a brief CV appended. I spent a Sunday afternoon following these instructions, stripping down my public service-style CV to look more like a résumé and writing a letter. My letter was very straightforward; it comprised seven paragraphs. The first paragraph stated my wish to register my application for the post. The last paragraph provided a very brief summary of my reasons for being interested in the post, my hope that the letter was clear and helpful, and my hope that I may be able to expand upon it at interview. The five paragraphs in the middle were simply one to each criterion in the Specification, giving a brief example or other evidence to show that I could meet their needs. The letter ran to about two and a half pages, with the normal letter headings and layout. To cut a long story short, I was longlisted but didn't take things beyond that point. However, I later asked the HR Director for some feedback on my application. She told me that I was one of the first people on the longlist – not because I was an early applicant, but because I had done exactly what they asked and provided the evidence to show that I met their criteria. I was amazed, as the post was not really in my field, and I said, 'But, surely, everyone did the same, didn't they?' Her reply was, 'Tom, don't be so naive – hardly anyone followed the instructions!' I guess that the longlisting for that post did not take too long!

## Some things to avoid

In addition to not following basic instructions, there are some other gaffs to avoid.

- Sending in a paper copy of your CV with a covering of either a 'Post-it' note or a small sheet of lilac-coloured paper instead of a more formal letter probably won't go down too well. I've seen such notes stuck on, just saying 'Re – your ad in last week's XYZ'.

- Don't put crucial information about your candidacy into the covering letter without also putting it into your CV – unless it is asked for, as in my personal example. Often, in larger organisations the covering letters don't make it to the interviewers, being set aside in the HR or photocopy office.

- If you use a standard CV – especially of the résumé style – do print it off fresh each time you use it, on decent quality paper. Fourth-generation photocopies never look as attractive as an original. The worst example I've ever seen was from a very senior person, who really should have known a lot better. He sent in a 17-page standard CV, which had obviously been photocopied over and again. It was completely unedited and unstructured for the job (a CEO position!) and the ancient photocopying meant that many pages did not line up properly. It was a very interesting read – his life and career story, in effect – but he didn't make it to the shortlist.

- Don't try to be funny – unless you know your audience personally very well indeed and know that they will appreciate the joke.

- Unless it is specifically requested, it is probably better not to include photographs of yourself or gimmicks such as images from Clip Art. The former, unfortunately, can be used critically (unless you are incredibly photogenic), as employers may make judgements about you from your appearance in the picture, which you are not there in person to correct. The latter can look tacky and give an impression that you're desperate to show off your computer skills – or, worse still, that you need to fill up empty space because you have nothing useful to say. Obviously, as with many of these principles, there may be exceptions. For example, in a 'creative' industry or job, something unusual or even artistic might be appreciated. Think carefully about whether this employer/position is one of those exceptions, before you do anything that might otherwise be written off as gimmicky.

- Avoid the commercially available off-the-shelf CVs that are around. I've tried to make it clear that I think that CVs should be personal, customised statements. If you use a pre-prepared CV, you will risk cutting across all of this advice around customising your CV to yourself and to the industry/organisation. I suggest also that you will not be sending in your CV, even if it has some of your details in it, but in reality someone else's. You also run the risk of the employer recognising the version you are using and being less than impressed.

## Finding the right job opportunity

In this chapter, I have assumed that you might be preparing your CV, résumé or application form for a specific post, or at least for a specific organisation or industry to which you may send your CV speculatively (what I've called sending in a CV 'cold'). However, in this final section, I want to say a little about looking out for these opportunities and positioning yourself.

I have stressed several times the importance of being yourself and looking for a post that matches your skills, experience, ambitions and style. Thus, if you are already happily into a profession, industry or type of job, then the two basic approaches you need to consider if moving onwards and upwards are firstly keeping in touch with the posts being advertised and secondly seeking out organisations with possible vacancies that are not yet on the open market.

For the first of these two approaches, you need to find out what are the standard publications, newsletters, vacancy bulletins or websites in which the type of posts you are seeking will be advertised. If you are really actively seeking a move, then you may need to consider taking out subscriptions to professional or trade journals, to ensure that you don't miss out. Additionally, you may need to spend time regularly visiting either general employment websites or the websites of specific organisations, in order to keep in touch.

Once you spot an opportunity, remember to find out all you can about the post and employer – either by sending for information packs or by doing some research of your own. All of this will support your customising of your CV to ensure that the employer believes that you have something to offer.

If you are considering sending in a CV 'cold', I would still strongly suggest doing the research and homework. Employers and recruitment companies receive many such 'cold' CVs. You therefore need to ensure that yours does not just get discarded or filed away. So, you should consider what they are likely to be looking for (again, from trade journals and websites, find out what are their big issues at present) and how can you best demonstrate that you have something unique or desirable.

If you are not even at the stage yet of looking for specific posts or organisations, perhaps because you are thinking of a complete career change, you need to start your research and homework even further back. You need to think in the way that a school-leaver or new graduate would. Ask yourself some of these questions:

- What do I really enjoy doing?
- What am I good at doing?
- Am I prepared to train/retrain – with the possible consequences on earnings in the short term?
- Do I want responsibility or leadership roles or am I happy as a team member/worker?
- What sort of career development opportunities do I want – do I want a straightforward 'job for life' or am I looking for a position that could take me upwards and outwards?
- What do I want/need in terms of salary and benefits?
- Do I have/want geographical limits on where I work?
- Do I need a job that gives me a particular work-life balance?
- Then finally, where might I compromise on the balances between enjoyment, satisfaction, pay, geography, career and other life issues?

My strong advice is to find the type of support that school-leavers and graduates have in terms of careers advisers. Obviously, this does not have to be a formal career adviser, but could be provided by family members, friends and colleagues. However, do not forget the potential availability of specialist careers advisers at your local Employment Centre or at a recruitment company or agency. Further, don't be afraid to approach people in the type of professions, jobs or organisations that may be of interest to you. My experience is that they are usually flattered to be asked to talk about their jobs, careers or professions and will often give you much more time than you might have imagined. In one of my former roles as a hospital manager, I was approached many times by students, members of the public and members of the hospital's clinical and support staff about careers and opportunities in hospital management. I don't think that I ever turned down anyone who asked to have time to talk these things over with me.

**Further reading**

As I mentioned at the start of this chapter, there are plenty of books telling you how to prepare your CV. I'm wary of some of them, for the reasons I've already stated. However, I would recommend the following very accessible and easy-to-use books. They include more examples and model layouts than we have space to give you here, they are published in the UK and they do not try to preach only one way of preparing a CV:

Eggert, M. (1999) *The Perfect CV* (London, Random House Business Books).

Howard, S. (1999) *Creating a Successful CV* (London, Dorling Kindersley).

## Note

1. I'm assuming here that we are considering professional, technical and managerial posts, for which the use of a CV as the means of imparting your personal, educational, professional and other information is likely. For clerical, manual and other such jobs, the use of a pre-printed application form telling you exactly what the employer wants and where to put it on the form, is probably more likely. Having said that, at least some of the suggestions in this chapter could usefully be applied to an application form.

# Chapter 3
## Interview Intelligence

**Tom Storrow**

### Introduction

Interviews can create all manner of nervous reactions – not least amongst those doing the interviewing! I can think of many situations throughout my own career, particularly when fairly junior staff were involved on either side of the interview table, when it was unclear who was the most nervous, interviewer or interviewee.

Why is this so? My guess is that this may be one of the most formal yet personal interactions that people have at work. Obviously, much can be riding on the interview for all concerned and everyone wants to look and sound good. If you haven't had much experience as interviewer/interviewee, it can be a potentially nerve-wracking time.

In this chapter, I shall concentrate on trying to provide some tips for the interviewees, but some of the observations and suggestions may be equally valid for those of you doing the interviewing. Similarly, I have tried to focus on recruitment-type interviews, but again some of the comments will be applicable in other interview situations, such as those for appraisals, research or even investigations or disciplinary matters.

My tips are based on a mixture of research of the varied literature, personal experience, observation, and – I hope – some common sense. Some of them will seem very obvious, having been stated in almost every guide to interviews ever written, but they do bear repetition. Others may seem almost crass, and you will think, 'Surely no one would ever do that!' However, unfortunately, all are based on real examples of bad practices as well as good.

I'll start with some general comments that could apply to virtually any interview format, but as I go on I will try to describe some of the different formats and some specific things that you can consider for each. The final section touches on some of the different interview settings and some issues to look out for before and after the interview itself.

## Interview tips

### Influencing the interview through your CV

You can start your influencing of the interview when you prepare your CV. As indicated in the last chapter, full CVs should always be tailored to the post or industry, based upon your research about them and then deploying carefully your evidence, experiences and skills. However, this can be done in such a way as to suggest areas for expansion and follow-up at interview. Leave 'hooks' on which the panel can hang some questions. For example, on some notable experiences tell them briefly what you achieved, but do not tell them how – save that for the interview.

This is much easier with the shorter, résumé style of CV. Here, you will only have space to give a very basic outline of the jobs you have held and your skills and experiences in them – this should always be developed at the interview and meeting stages.

### Presentations at the start of an interview

Many of the more formal type of interviews – especially in the public and academic sectors – now start with a presentation, so remember some of the key tactics for good presentations:

- Keep to time – there is nothing worse than over-running badly and having the Interview Panel Chair stop your presentation. For a 10-minute presentation, aim to finish in say 9 to 9 and a half minutes, and rehearse this.
- Avoid jokes as part of your 'warm-up' – they rarely work.
- If you are allowed visual aids, such as PowerPoint or overhead projector, then use the minimum number of slides, each with the minimum number

of words on them – in such a pressured situation you want simple reinforcement and summarisation, not complex lists or analyses. Similarly, I suggest avoiding the fancy 'transitions' on PowerPoint, as they can distract from the simple messages of reinforcement and summary that you are trying to get across in a limited time.

- If you are using an overhead projector put the slides into protective covers, to make them easier to handle.

- You should never use paper 'windows' over parts of an OHP slide, and nor should you ever try to cover parts of a slide with a loose piece of paper – if you need to reveal a slide's contents in stages, then you have put too much information on it (obviously, this is much easier to handle with a PowerPoint presentation).

- Rehearse the physical side of the presentation aids – setting up and using the PowerPoint projector or OHP. (Incidentally, for my own presentations, I now tend to take my laptop, assuming that the venue will have projection facilities for PowerPoint, plus OHP slides as back-up, and printed copies of the slides in case both technologies fail! The worst case of PowerPoint failure I've seen, with the candidate struggling on and on to try to get the system and his own presentation working, went on for 17 minutes, by which time any attempt to continue was only wasting everyone's time.)

- Face your audience, not the screen, and make eye contact with all of them from time-to-time. Try to avoid using notes, other than perhaps a single card with your 'prompts' on it – and certainly avoid reading your presentation word-by-word. All of these things will help you to make more eye contact and to raise your head from out of the notes and slides.

- Try to use the 'rule of threes' – basing your presentation around three broad themes, each with three sub-points.

- Remember the old teachers' adage: (a) tell them what you are going to tell them, (b) tell them, and (c) then tell them what you have told them.

- The use of the last two points could give you a simple format to follow in a 10 minute presentation – a few seconds with an introductory slide to tell them of your three key themes; a maximum of 3 minutes on each theme, covering three sub-points for up to 1 minute each, and with a slide for each theme (the slide should have just three lines on it, one for each of the sub-points); 20 seconds to summarise and tell them what you have told them, with a repeat of your introductory slide (total 9 to 9 and a half minutes).

- If you are prone to fidgeting whilst on your feet making presentations, then you must prepare yourself to try to stop this. I usually tell men to take their keys and change out of their pockets before they go into the interview room. Women are much less likely to have pockets full of keys and money, but they can just as easily fidget with their jewellery – so dress carefully. Other points about body language are covered later in the chapter.

The same broad rules and structures will work for other types of recruitment presentations, such as those to groups of potential colleagues, stakeholders or staff.

### *Entrances and where and how to sit*

The first thing to be aware of here is to manage your entrance to the room. Try to think about whether you are likely to be greeted at the door and offered handshakes, or alternatively just told to come in and take a seat. If you don't know how they will handle this, then be prepared for anything that might face you as you enter, so that you can concentrate on eye contact and positive first impressions, rather than being surprised or looking around for what to do. Similarly, leave bags and cases outside if at all possible – as you enter, you should be focused on the interviewer(s) not on where to leave your bags.

In the main part of a formal interview, try to sit where you can make eye contact with each panel member without having to do much more than move your eyes or your head and upper body. If the chair they have given to you is too close to the desk or table, then move it back a little as you sit down, so that you can see everyone without moving too much. Do not move your chair to face different members of the panel at different times through the interview (I've seen that done four or five times!). Furthermore, never put your elbows on the interview desk/table (I've seen that done three times – on each occasion, the interviewers shrank back from the invasion of their – or least the neutral – space).

If you are in a boardroom, meeting room or someone's office, you will have to take the chair set out for you. However, if you are around a coffee table or if there is just you and the interviewer in a meeting room, then try to pick a seat where you will sit across a corner of the table from the interviewer, rather than on opposite sides of the table. This can feel more comfortable; perhaps a little more like a discussion between colleagues.

### *Body position and gestures*

There are plenty of writers much better qualified than I am to write in detail about body language or non-verbal communication. However, as an experienced interviewer and interviewee, perhaps I can suggest a few basics to look out for.

The first thing to try to do is what is often called 'positive listening', when you make eye contact with the person speaking to you, and smile and nod at appropriate points. This is remarkably effective in getting people to be positive about you and to pay you more attention. Try it out in a meeting or at a smallish lecture – you might be surprised at how much the speakers will start to focus on you, as they receive signals telling them that you are interested, supportive and attentive.

Next, think about your posture. You need to be comfortable, so that you won't be wriggling in your seat after 15 minutes, but you also need to look alert and attentive. As I said in the first section, I've seen this carried to extremes, with candidates placing their elbows on the table or on their knees as they lean forward and try to look intense and engaged. This usually looks at best rather false and at worst will give signals of aggression ('invading their space') to the interviewers. Think about where you put your feet as well as your hands. Shuffling, bouncy feet can be a real indicator of nerves, whilst obviously your hands can be a real help or hindrance. Try to keep your hands fairly still and usually together, using them occasionally if you want to give a non-verbal signal of emphasis, balance, etc. Clearly, wringing hands, playing with jewellery, flailing arms or tightly crossed arms all give fairly obvious signals.

If you are in a boardroom, you may be able to hide nervous feet and hands under the table for at least some of the time. If you are in an armchair or round a coffee table, this will be impossible, so you must be aware of your own nervous habits and try to control them.

### *Listen carefully to the questions*

Listen carefully to the questions that are being asked of you and let the questioner finish the question. This doesn't just mean that you should appear to be listening through the 'positive listening' signals – you really do need to hear what is being said and asked. In particular, you need to be aware of falling into the trap of hearing and responding to a 'trigger word' in the first line of a question by telling them everything you know about it at great length. As I cover in more detail later, don't be afraid to clarify a question or take a few seconds to think about your response.

## Is the interviewer listening?

Remember the concept of something I've heard called 'mental noise'. Often, after someone has spoken – for example in asking you a rather complex question – they will be re-running their own words in their head for a few moments, asking themselves, 'Did I phrase that correctly?' During this time, they may not be listening to you as intently as you might wish. So, if you are confused by the question, pause and ask politely for clarification – to help you and them. If you are not confused but you are concerned with whether they are listening properly, start your answer with a brief 'holding statement', such as, 'That's an interesting question…' or 'Yes, I did read the report on that matter…' (Obviously, you can also use this tactic to buy a few moments thinking time – but don't over-use it, as interviewers will quickly get wise.)

## How should I answer 'big' or wide-ranging questions?

If you are asked very wide-ranging questions, try to give 'headline' answers, which demonstrate that you know and understand the issues, but through which you can then invite them to ask you to expand. For example, if you are asked about a major or even rather philosophical subject that we will call 'XYZ', you could begin by saying something such as: 'XYZ is a very big issue in our work and I'm sure that we could all give a lengthy lecture on it. However, to me, the key components of XYZ are ABC and the key financial components of this, DEF and its training implications, and GHI and the marketing issues.' (You might add a few more words on each of these.) You can then ask the interviewer, 'Would you like me to expand on any of those points?'

Again, don't imagine that they want to hear everything you know on a subject in great detail – demonstrate that you understand the big picture and then see if they want you to go into more detail. Also, allowing them to ask you to expand makes them feel that they are in control of the interview, when in fact you are!

## How should I answer 'closed' questions?

On the other hand, you need to avoid one word or other extremely brief answers, unless these are very obviously called for. Sometimes, of course, interviewers are not very skilled and they ask you 'closed' questions, such as

'Racial discrimination in employment is wrong, isn't it?' Really, there should be a single word answer to this. However, if you think that they really meant to ask you, 'How would you go about handling an apparent case of racial discrimination within your department?' then you may again need to seek clarification about what they really want from you. This is much better than stunning them with a one word answer when they expected two minute's worth of considered response, or vice versa.

### *Use real and personal examples*

Whenever possible, deploy some personal evidence and experiences in order to show that you have done more than just 'read the book'. For professional and managerial posts, it is particularly important that you demonstrate, through both an intellectual understanding and some real experience, that you can do what they need you to do. Concrete examples in which you are personally involved are always the best evidence – it allows them to get to grips with a real example and provides you with the comfort of being on some home territory upon which you can easily expand if needed.

### *Use positive words and statements*

Try to use positive and active words and statements. For example, it sounds much better to say, 'I can deliver this project, based upon my previous experience with XYZ', as opposed to 'I think that I will be able to deliver the project as I once did something similar'. As I said in the CV chapter, never tell lies or claim something that isn't yours – the costs of being discovered are too great and the risks of being stressed by a job that you shouldn't really be in just aren't worth it. However, it is quite reasonable for you to stress the positives and to try to answer gaps by referring to alternative experiences or how you have handled and coped with a similar gap elsewhere.

Another good example of always staying positive lies in the classic answer to the old fallback question of tired interviewers, 'What are your weaknesses?' I learnt a long time ago that this is one of the easiest questions to answer, as long as you are prepared for it. Don't go for some glib answer such as, 'I suppose that my weakness is being sufficiently arrogant to believe that I don't have any other weaknesses!' Pick something that has been a weakness in the past, mention this and then go on to say how you have learnt to cope with it and turn it to your advantage. For example, 'Well, early in my career, one of my bosses used to tell me that I could appear rather driven and thus tended to judge others by my own standards. I came to realise that people can have very different motivators – and of course a range of other responsibilities outside of their career — and I began to do a little studying around this. It's helped me to explain what I want more clearly and to investigate what support my people may need to help them deliver it. That original feedback has been very helpful in improving my abilities as a manager.' Think of your own version of this and use it — you will rarely be asked for a second 'weakness'. (If you are, give a very quick second answer, such as, 'My numeracy skills are a little weaker than my written work, but I've learnt to handle this through close working with my departmental accountant colleagues.' You will almost never be asked for a third!)

### *Language*

Do some research into the type of language that is commonly used at the organisation and think about how and whether you can fit in with this. By language here I mean the organisational jargon or their manner of speaking.

Are they very formal, referring to people by their titles and surnames or are they informal, using all first names? Are they very strong on technical jargon? Are there any current organisational buzzwords or issues that everyone will be talking about? (This tends to happen in my field, the NHS, where new policies or reports are immediately referred to by an abbreviation or by the name of the person who chaired the committee producing the report — I'm sure you can think of examples from any organisation.) Will informal or 'street' language be frowned upon or encouraged? You might find that you can use slightly different styles of language depending upon the setting — for example, being more formal in the boardroom but speaking (still under control) a little less formally in a one-to-one with a potential colleague.

### *Dress*

Dress codes for interviews have to reflect the type of post and organisation involved. It is probably best to go for standard business attire for most professional and managerial posts, although there will be exceptions to this — perhaps, for example, if you are applying for a job with a creative or computing company, where dress might be much less formal.

The obvious rules must be to check out what appears to be the dress code in that organisation, but if in doubt you should go for a 'default position' of smart business wear. Generally, darker colours appear more sober and professional, whilst very bright colours usually look like the wearer is trying to make a statement. Jewellery should also be smart and understated.

Remember that most managers doing the interviewing are likely to be of an age, background or seniority that may have a bearing on their impressions of you. Similarly, the post for which you are being interviewed may have particular requirements in terms of appearance. For example, an applicant for either a Receptionist post or a new Partner post with a firm of county-town lawyers who turns up with nose-rings, pink hair, a bare midriff or wearing combat gear might not impress!

For more on appearance and personal presentation, see Chapter 5.

### *Preparation and 'question-spotting'*

It is quite possible to prepare for an interview in much the same way as we all did for our exams at school, by 'question-spotting' (and also by 'panel-spotting'). You should be able to work out some of the most likely key question areas from any role and person specifications made available to you, and/or from any visits you have made to the organisation, plus other intelligence gathering. For example, if numeracy and financial management appear high up the Person Specification, whilst budget management is a key part of the Role Specification, then you really should expect some questions about your budgeting experience and your numeracy. (You may also find that they will wish to carry out assessments of your skills through formal tests as part of the selection process.) Similarly, if there are less tangible issues that do not appear openly in the Specifications, but which are obvious on a visit and which the organisation fairly readily admits, such as issues around team-working, a merger or new technology, then again you should expect and prepare for questions on this.

Similarly, look at who will be on the panel. This is probably easier in the public sector, where the panel membership is likely to be made known to you. Try to find out about their particular interests or pet subjects. Both of these will enable you to predict at least some of the questions, so that you can prepare your answers.

### *Pauses and silences*

Don't be afraid occasionally to pause for a few seconds for thought, and don't panic when you do so. Used carefully, a pause for thought can make you look thoughtful and considered. However, I'm sure that most of us think that a few seconds silence in an interview feels like several minutes and this can easily panic us into saying something (anything!) to fill the space.

If you are really struggling to say something, use the 'holding statements' I mentioned earlier and/or ask politely for some clarification. For example, you can say, 'That's a really big question for our whole industry/me/our profession, do you want me to give you my personal impressions on the subject or to discuss the current national policy position?' Something like this will again give you some thinking time, but it will also allow you to find out exactly what the interviewer was looking for, without you appearing either too challenging or ignorant.

If you really don't know the answer to a question, then it is always better to say so, rather than holding a really prolonged silence – or, worse still, waffling on and proving that you don't know the answer! In my experience, interviewers tend to be more impressed by someone being honest than by someone trying to con them!

### *Aggressive interviewers*

I'm sometimes asked how to handle an aggressive interviewer. I think that the first issue to decide is whether this aggression is a role that the interviewer has been asked to play, for example to test candidates' resilience under pressure. This might be acceptable for some posts.

However, if you think that this isn't a role that they are playing, then you need to think about how much you want the job and whether you are prepared to accept aggressive and/or patronising questions and comments. If the employer/company accepts or even encourages aggressive, patronising or possibly discriminatory behaviours, then you will just have to accept this and respond either in kind or as positively as you can, if you do really want the job. (In these circumstances, Martin Higham recommends imagining the interviewer sitting in his or her bath!) Otherwise, withdraw from the selection process and look elsewhere.

### *Any questions for them?*

Often, at the end of an interview, you will be asked if you have any questions. In a larger, formal interview setting, the best answer is something like, 'No, thank you, I've had the opportunity to clarify the things that I needed to clarify before the interview. Thank you for inviting me to come along today'. If you haven't had the opportunity for discussions and clarification, then either you haven't tried hard enough, or if you have tried but they haven't answered, then you need to ask yourself, 'Why?' and 'Do I want to work for such an organisation?' Never,

ever produce a list of questions you want to work through – it makes the panel's hearts sink!

It may be more appropriate for you to ask questions in a less formal, perhaps one-to-one interview, where a genuine exchange of information is being sought. If you are in one of these settings – perhaps at an early stage in the process or with a less formal employer – then you should have prepared a few key questions that are important to you.

However, if you are asked whether there are any additional or closing comments that you wish to make, then don't pass up this opportunity in any setting. Max Eggert recommends that you have a 30-word statement prepared about yourself to use in these situations, to sum up your abilities and why they should appoint you. You should certainly have something ready for these opportunities and combine them with a brief and pleasant 'thank you for inviting me' sentence. Remember that first and last impressions really can make a big difference, and a good closing statement can leave the panel/interviewer with a favourable impression as you leave.

### *Salary negotiations*

You should not introduce pay negotiation into an interview, unless you are in the type of one-to-one final interview where pay is clearly part of the agenda. If you are in a panel interview situation and the pay/package is an issue for you, then you should raise it in principle before the interview, and then discuss it after an offer has been made. Apart from anything else, once an offer has been made, you are in a much stronger position to negotiate, as the organisation is unlikely to want to let you go and start the recruitment process all over again!

## Some specific interview types and events around the interview itself

### *Interview and assessment settings*

I can think of many different types or settings for a recruitment interview, such as:

- A formal interview (i.e. you and them on opposite sides of the boardroom table or at least a large desk) before a panel of senior managers and assessors.
- A formal interview before just one or two senior managers.
- A formal interview before the owner of the company on his/her own.
- An informal (i.e. 'round the coffee table' version) of most of the above.

- A series of two or three shorter, 'criteria-based' interviews, in which you will be seen by different small panels or individuals who will each be looking at different criteria from the employer's specifications for the post.

- Longer, probably less formal interviews with recruitment consultants who have been retained by the employer to search out or assess candidates for a final shortlist.

- Meetings, presentations and interviews with potential colleagues, staff, board members or other 'stakeholders'. These can range from presentations to a large number of colleagues and/or staff to apparently informal one-to-one 'chats' – but all should be regarded as part of the interview and assessment process.

- Apparently 'social' interactions, including the traditional 'trial by sherry'.

All of these types – and I'm sure that you will be able to add several variations or new types – of interview or assessment should be regarded as requiring you to be 'on parade'. I've seen people blow their chances by saying or doing something inappropriate in an off-guard moment during apparently more informal or social events. For example, a male candidate who took off his jacket and tie and drank mineral water from the bottle during a fairly formal 'trial by sherry'; and a female candidate who said something rude about one panel member to another during an informal one-to-one.

## *Handling the 'social events'*

Before moving on to touch on some other potential aspects of the selection process, I'd like to say a little more about these apparently social events. As I've already said, you should regard every part of the face-to-face contact as being part of the assessment – and this should even include asides made to the person showing you in and out of the interview room or to and from reception (don't forget how important the opinions of the MD's secretary may be!).

Being 'on parade' means that you should try to avoid eating or drinking during most of these events – apart from at sit-down meals, although even then I'd aim to eat as little as politely possible. Be very wary of buffets and drinks – carry round a plate with a sandwich on it and keep a half-glass of water in your hand in case you need a sip, but otherwise plan to eat after the event. The dangers lie, of course, in spilling/dropping things and in being asked questions whilst you have a mouth full of vol-au-vent.

I extend the eating and drinking cautions into the interview room itself. If possible, avoid drinks and biscuits – again, other than a half-glass of water. Full glasses, cups and saucers and biscuit crumbs have an amazing ability to empty themselves all over candidates at the worst possible moment. For example, be careful of small bottles of sparkling mineral water – I once saw an unchilled bottle go off, in the hands of the candidate trying to open it, like a champagne bottle on a Grand Prix rostrum! Similarly, even if the coffee or tea offered to you doesn't spill, the slightest hand tremor can be exaggerated by a cup and saucer, suggesting a nervousness that you want to hide.

### *Other potential parts of the assessment process*

However, there can be other stages to a selection process as well as the interview itself and these social events. I have mentioned already the use of assessment techniques such as tests and profiling, but these are worthy of further consideration.

Tests of numerical, verbal and non-verbal reasoning and ability, plus personality questionnaires are used for some senior, professional or technical posts. Sometimes these are combined together with interviews and group exercises into an Assessment Centre. The purpose of this multi-faceted approach is to obtain a wide range of possible evidence about the candidates' abilities, style, experience and potential.

If you are going to be asked to undertake either a full Assessment Centre or some tests and profiles alongside a more standard interview, then this will normally be made clear to you in advance. This should allow you to prepare yourself, at least of the level of gaining some familiarity with the techniques to be used.

If you are already inside a larger organisation, you may be able to get access to some of the standard tests, exercises and profiles from your in-house training or human resources department. If you do not have such support, you can access many examples via the Internet. For example, my company often uses the tests and profiles developed by Saville and Holdsworth Ltd, one of the major suppliers in the UK – you can find out about them, their techniques and samples via the SHL website.

It is important to remember that some of these techniques are tests, whilst others are not. The numeracy papers, for example, will test your abilities, usually giving you a percentile score against a comparable cohort of managers or operatives. On the other hand, personality questionnaires do not have right and wrong answers – only your answers. They are designed to ask you to give preferences against a range of statements or issues, with the collated answers indicating your style, motivations, attitudes and so on. Most of the major personality questionnaires are sufficiently well designed and validated to detect attempts to skew the profile or give a false impression, so don't be tempted to try to give answers that you think the employer wants. As in the CV and the interview, be yourself – if they like it, that's great and if they don't then that's great as well.

Occasionally you may also be asked to participate in group exercises. These may take the form of a debate or discussion by candidates around a series of issues or options. Usually, they are again used to get an indication of style, listening, influence and decision-making. The best tactic is simply to participate positively, being aware of the impact that you have on others and the task assigned to you. Remember to consider what the assessors might be looking for; it might be power and persuasiveness or it might be skills in involving others and reaching a consensus.

## Conclusion

Do remember that when your CV has 'opened the door' to a prospective employer, you then have to go through the door and sell yourself, showing them why they should appoint you. Everything that you say, do and wear can have an impact on the overall impression that you make, so think carefully and ensure that the version of you that they see is a well-prepared, true and positive one.

## Further reading

As in the case of CVs, there are plenty of books around to advise you about presentations and interviews further and in more detail than we can here. Two that I have found helpful and accessible are:

Eggert, M. (1999) *The Perfect Interview* (London, Random House Business Books).

Higham, M. (1983) *Coping with Interviews* (London, New Opportunity Press).

# Chapter 4
## Salaries and Individual Performance Reviews

**Jennifer Parr**

### Introduction

It has to be said that I never considered myself an expert on salaries and individual performance reviews. Like many of us, when faced with the opportunity to move jobs or go for that next promotion I found the conversation with prospective employers to determine the salary very awkward, and I always wished that there was some quick advice, a formula to follow, or time to research it properly. I'd get through the ordeal, and emerge with a sense of achievement or 'I should have gone for more' feeling. Likewise in my experience individual performance review/appraisals differ from organisation-to-organisation, and significance from role-to-role. I have never been offered training or advice on preparation. Therefore, the whole experience can become quite confusing, and meant that my performance in the appraisal is not likely to be effective.

In my endeavour to produce some tips for you, I have learnt an immense amount about the traps and trends that we as women share at national and international levels. Hopefully, in compiling this, we will all be enlightened and forewarned. It should also allow us to become more aware of the context that we find ourselves in, and therefore more competent in our quest to avoid them.

## Salaries

### *Legislation and Policy*

'The Equal Pay Act (1970) requires women to show that they do work or are work rated as equivalent by a job evaluation scheme, or work of equal value to that of a male comparator'[1]. At the turn of the century, 30 years after the Act, women are still receiving £250,000 less than equivalently qualified men over their career (Walsh, 2000). David Harper suggests that the Kingsmill Report (December, 2001) on women's employment and pay does not go far enough to overturn ingrained discriminatory practice as there is a reluctance to legislate for change.

### The gender pay gap – women and unequal pay

Perhaps naively, I had assumed that the world was fair, and that regardless of gender, I would be remunerated according to my ability and performance. After all, this is the twenty-first century. However, there is a gender pay gap, which is hugely complex, resulting in women earning only 82% of the average male salary when engaged in full-time work, and only 61% when part-time[2]. The gender pay gap is analysed at national and international level, and the contributing factors in the UK cannot be assumed to be the same in Europe, America or the developing world. I don't propose to unravel the full picture, but rather to whet the appetite by providing insight into the gender pay gap, which will inform your preparation in the context of any prospective job.

The *Final Report to the Women and Equality Unit* (Anderson *et al.*, 2001) endeavoured to understand the causes of the gender pay gap. These are in summary:

- Women have less work experience than men, and more part-time experiences, which are rewarded less favourably.
- Part-time working is overwhelmingly concentrated amongst women.
- Women tend to spend less time commuting than men, possibly due to the predominance of caring being accomplished by women, employed in part-time roles, and taking up employment nearer to home. This may lead to a higher incidence of lower paid women in an area, driving down the wage for women-concentrated jobs.
- Female-dominated occupations are often the lowest paid.
- Undervaluing of women occurs through appraisal systems, reward systems, retention measures, wage setting practices and valuation of 'women's work'.

Public sector employment provides evidence of a smaller gender pay gap. Women earn 92% of their male counterparts average salary when in full-time employment compared with 72% when part-time. Teaching and nursing are predominantly female dominated professions and are provided by the public sector. Women in the private sector tend to earn between 3 and 5% less than those in the public sector.

## Unpaid labour

What is 'work' then? Many definitions have been used over time. In the 1930s Margaret Reid developed the third party principle to account for what constitutes domestic production. That is those tasks, which a third party could perform for pay (cited Benería [1999]).

Benería (1999) describes the complexities of the debate over unpaid labour, and argues that internationally governments do not collect accurate statistics or effectively acknowledge the contribution made by those working part-time, or in unpaid contexts. The result on an international level is that the GNP of countries is not accurate. This is an example of the consequences of ignoring the contribution of women and their labours. She divides the contribution of unpaid work into three areas:

*1. Subsistence sector*

The estimation of backyard rural household activities like cultivation of vegetables as well as those of subsistence production in agriculture, forestry and fishing. Women's unpaid agricultural labour is highly integrated with domestic activities (Benería, 1999, p.290). This is more prevalent in developing countries, with the resulting effect on the inaccurate calculation of GNP.

*2. The household economy*

Assessment of the contribution of domestic work is totally excluded as it falls outside conventional definitions of work. As women provide most of the domestic work, this exclusion affects predominantly women.

*3. Volunteer work*

These tasks are not directly linked to the market, it is often of a professional nature and increasingly provided by women, and those with particular social characteristics.

The Cabinet Office report showed that women do take more time out from conventional paid work than men, and on average have 4 years less work experience than men. It appeared that absence from the labour market for 4 years significantly affected the returning salary, however there was no real effect for periods longer than 4 years[3]. Women were particularly affected if they were absent from the labour market for more than four years if the reason was to undertake further education, whereas their male counterparts were unaffected.

A study undertaken to assess the effect of childbearing (twins) on married women's labour supply and earnings concluded that in the short-term, childbearing does reduce women's participation in the labour market. Surprisingly, the impact of unplanned births on labour market participation has begun to decrease over the longer term (Jacobsen *et al.*, 1999).

**Negotiating salaries**

As mentioned earlier, I found the salary negotiation element of a job move quite awkward, perhaps I felt it was a bit 'bad taste' to talk about money. As a result I have fallen into all the traps of what 'not' to do over the years. I was always puzzled about when was the right time to bring it up and how much should I go for.

On one occasion, throughout the interview process, the only thing I knew about the salary was what it said in the advertisement, which led me to believe that the company would offer a fair salary. When it came time to have the discussion, I was naive and unprepared to negotiate. I had been led to believe I should be grateful for the job, I accepted less than I was worth and the experience set the scene for the forthcoming employment. My self-esteem was directly affected by the outcome, and therefore my personality and performance as well.

Chastain (1980) starts her book, by suggesting in the preface:

*'... by negotiating, women stop discriminating against themselves and increase their earnings in the process'.*

What is negotiation then? Negotiation is not a confrontation, but it is a dialogue between two parties (at least) to agree some mutual accommodation. When you negotiate, the outcome should be a win-win situation for both parties.

Chastain devotes a whole book to the topic of negotiation of salaries and although it is now over 20 years old, it's value is very current, and its concepts fit closely with best practice.

## How to get the best salary

### *Choices*

Easily the most important thing to remember about negotiating a salary is that you must do it. There is really no choice. This is part of the process for men and women to advance themselves and there is no reason why women should allow men to get all the spoils.

Certain choices are available about how and when to do it. Chastain advises to wait until the end of the interview process, and when you are sure you have a job offer, as by this time, you will have had an opportunity to learn about what is important to the employer, and you can use this to demonstrate how you meet their requirements. Even if they raise it with you earlier, it is best to avoid the discussion until you have a chance to really appreciate what they want. She also suggests:

- Make the first offer. This lets the employer realise your expectations of salary.

- Don't accept straight away, as you may need time to reflect, and possibly come back with more questions regarding other benefits.

- Don't appear too eager. They must feel that they have worked hard to get you.

- Never undertake salary negotiation over the telephone, and I would extend this further to include more recent developments in technology, like email. Whilst it may feel more comfortable for you to be separated in time or place, it does not facilitate the nuances of communication that you need to be aware of. It is more in your interest to be face-to-face, as the employer is less likely to feel comfortable offering a low salary, if you are there in person to respond. Make an appointment to discuss the salary when the time is convenient to you, and when you have had ample time to prepare mentally.

### Practice and preparation

Even if you are not interested in the actual job, it is really helpful to get some practice without the added pressure of ruining your chances with the one job you really do want. Apply for a variety of jobs, and attend one or two interviews. Try to get as far in the process as possible, and practice the salary negotiation phase to gain familiarity.

A few years ago, I was looking to change jobs, and I went to a prestigious recruitment company to help me. Throughout the process I was coached at every stage. They also provide quite a lot of background information about the prospective employer, and can help you to identify a suitable salary range. They also provided some tips about presentation, both of myself, and throughout the interview. This included posture and how to appear interested but not aggressive. To demonstrate this, they conducted a mock interview, and judged me on my performance including non-verbals.

I was advised to do four things, all of which will influence how well you will do when it comes time to negotiate that salary:

- Prepare a written summary of myself demonstrating how I matched their requirements both in the job description and the brief I had been provided. Using the same terminology and phrases helps them visualise you within their organisation.

- Ask them if they had any concerns about my experience, or fit for the job in question. This gives them an opportunity to raise any last issues with you but more importantly, it provides you with the chance to reconcile their concerns and reinforce your strengths and match.

- Ask for the job! After all, you have already got them to confirm that they have no concerns about your experience, and therefore demonstrated that there is no reason why you should not be employed.

- Write a letter to them after the interview stating how you really benefited from the opportunity to meet with them, re-confirm your interest in the position, and reinforce your match with their specification.

These were unnatural behaviours for me as I would never normally be so aggressive to get what I want. But if it is not me demonstrating my worth to the prospective employer, then it will be my competition. Two of the hardest things to do involved handing over the summary at the end of the interview, and asking for the job. I have done this three times in my career and have got the job each time. It helped the interviewer see several things about me.

- The quality of my work
- My dedication to get what I wanted
- How closely I matched their requirements.

By the time it came to talking about money, they really wanted me, and could not see how others they had interviewed would help them achieve their aims as effectively.

Prepare answers to likely questions or situations. Put yourself in the situation of the employer, and focus on what they feel are essential qualities. The job description will provide this information, but consider other personal qualities to assist you to calculate your value to the organisation.

Practice the conversation using role-play, anticipating and preparing their objections to the salary you perceive to be reasonable. This helps you become more comfortable using the words, hearing yourself speak in a positive objective way about your strengths rather than focussing on your weaknesses.

**Deciding your value**

Undertake some benchmarking. Find out about other organisations with similar roles. You could explore this in the interview, or contact other organisations directly. Determine what the salary ranges are for the role, and how the role you are applying for differs in its scope, and responsibility. Assess the ranges both within the private and public sector, as we have seen there are marked differences in salaries between the two.

Calculate the amount you need to earn in order to live in the manner that you intend to. This should be the lowest salary you would accept. Hopefully, this will be somewhere within the salary range that you are anticipating.

Chastain has advice about how to pitch your price. She says to pitch it higher than the top of the range, in order to give you room to negotiate. The exact amount should be anywhere between 5–20% higher but this is a personal choice. Both parties need room to be flexible. You must expect to accept less than you ask for, and they must expect to pay more. Both of you must in the end feel that you have negotiated, and neither should feel that they have lost face.

This is where your earlier preparation comes to fruition, as you have not only already established their likely objections, but also answered them and developed your rationale for a higher salary, and why you are value for money to them.

**Other elements**

There are other factors, which will affect your decision about salary, and also about the suitability of the job for you. You must consider how are you going to advance in the future, both in terms of role and salary. This will involve a certain amount of research.

## How the salary is structured

There is evidence to show that women are more likely to work for small employers (Anderson *et al.*, 2001), are less likely to belong to a trade union, and as a result are unlikely to benefit from collective bargaining.

You may find that there are automatic annual increments which you are entitled to regardless of your performance, within a pay scale, or conversely you may be put on a salary which will not increase until you re-negotiate, or change positions. If this is the case, when you agree a salary, also agree a review date, and ensure that this is confirmed in writing.

## How are increases negotiated?

Are increases based on your performance and linked to an appraisal system, or does the organisation achieve this through collective bargaining with trade unions, or through job evaluations? Again, agree a date for an appraisal when you accept the position.

## Identify reward and incentive schemes

Some organisations conduct performance related pay (PRP) schemes. These should be non-discriminatory, and use formal systems to ensure equity.

## Contact the trade union

They will be able to advise you about the type of salary structure, and may even be able to give you advice about salary ranges.

## Promotion (pace and prospects)

Pudney and Shields (1999) stated that in the NHS, male nurses are promoted faster than their female colleagues, which amounts to up to £48,000 additional earnings over a career. It is therefore imperative to identify how other individuals have progressed. What are the prospects of promotion for you, how quickly is this likely, and how are promotions accessed. You could always speak to individuals who work there to appreciate their experiences, and also identify where the previous post holder has moved to.

Chastain makes a very valid point about negotiating future increases. Never dismiss the power of your current and day-to-day performance as a tool to negotiate that next salary, which she calls 'on the job negotiating'. Achieve maximum visibility within your role, as every positive stroke will be useful especially if you are dealing with senior colleagues. Undertake small challenges to lead projects, and utilise every opportunity to demonstrate by example your value to the organisation. This does not mean telling everyone how wonderful and indispensable you are, but making your contribution to the output of the organisation valid, especially with higher-level exposure.

**Individual Performance Review (IPR)**

Individual Performance Review (IPR) is one form of a personnel-based appraisal system, which is used widely in the public sector. Significantly women view their success differently from men in self-appraisal in that they are less likely to attribute it to their own ability[4]. The authors suggest that this influences the perceptions of the woman by male colleagues, and possibly provides barriers to progression (Andersen *et al.*, 2001). It is therefore necessary to appreciate the purpose, and process of IPR, in order that the disadvantages, which exist, are minimised, and maximum benefit can be obtained.

**Purpose**

There are several types of appraisal, which include competency-based and 360-degree appraisal. Whilst some forms of appraisal are purely organisation-based, Giddins and Turner (1995) suggest that appraisals typically comprise elements of both organisation and personnel-based approaches. They state the purpose of an appraisal system as being four-fold and based on the feedback loop:

1. Set standards

2. Monitor performance

3. Compare performance with the standards

4. Take action to improve.

Redman *et al.* (2000) categorise the outputs of the IPR system as those summarised in Table 1 below.

| Output | Explanation |
|---|---|
| Management Control | The setting and measuring of work objectives. |
| Employee Motivation | Enhanced job satisfaction and motivation as a result of face-to-face performance review.<br>* 66% of subjects in their study felt that the IPR contributed to improved job satisfaction and motivation. |
| Training and Development (Personal Development Plans) | The identification of training and development needs following performance review, as a result of clarifying strengths areas of development and specific objectives to achieve the development requirements.<br>* Although this is often discussed, this may be undertaken in a vague manner, and more emphasis placed on setting work objectives rather than developing a personal development plan.<br>* Often due to budgetary constraints employees were encouraged to find alternative development sources than costly courses. |
| Rewards (PRP) | Commonly IPR is linked to performance related pay (PRP). If this is the case, the IPR would result in a rating of an individual's performance, which would determine the reward, gained.<br>* The respondents did not favour the link between IPR and PRP. One of the criticisms was due to PRP being team dependant, but individually based. |

**Table 1.**

Appraisals often follow the yearly business planning process, and form part of the objective setting of the organisation. This process normally commences with the executive objective setting, and then cascades through senior managers and so on. Your place within the organisational structure will determine the time of the year when your appraisal will occur. The Labour Research Department (LRD) state that unions do not like links between appraisal and pay. However, increasingly IPR does link performance review with PRP. It is important to differentiate between the two however, and prevent any discrimination through arbitrary treatment of employees (LRD, 1990).

Most systems of appraisal will ensure that there is a formal process of preparation and review to achieve this. Ensure you are aware of anything your organisation provides to assist you and your employer to conduct a fair appraisal. The LRD also states that there should not be any negative consequences for you, if you are absent for example on maternity leave, jury or service or union activity.

Commonly an IPR will follow a pre-determined process within the organisation. There are several stages of the review[5]:

## Stage 1

### *Preparation*

- Reflect on your experience of appraisals, as this will assist you to put it into the context of your current organisation and appraisal system. This will also enable you to determine if you need any further explanation or training in the current system.

- Training should be provided both for you (the appraisee) and the appraiser to ensure that both of you are adequately prepared about the purpose, process and expectations of each role.

- Ensure that you agree a date for your review and the date is not re-scheduled. The existence of this will help you identify the commitment of the organisation to the appraisal system in place.

- You should consider and utilise any feedback provided by your manager regarding your performance within the previous year when performing your self-assessment.

### *Thinking about your personal development plan*

- Consider what you believe are important achievements for you in the next 12 months. This may be to develop further skills, for example, negotiation or people management.

- Attempt to decide what you want your next role to be, and any shortfall in your current skills. You may wish to meet managers of roles similar to one you wish to achieve, and discuss areas of development that will assist you in getting there.

- Some organisations and trade unions offer career counselling.

- Human resource departments can inform you of the essential criteria of your desired roles, and some can even provide assistance to demonstrate pathways to develop the skills and competencies required for individual positions.

*Pre-interview self-assessment form*

- Many organisations assist you in your preparation of an appraisal by providing a self-assessment form.

- This may provide questions and prompts to assist you to focus. It is generally not mandatory to share this with the appraiser. Common themes in this form could be[6]:
    - Satisfying aspects of the role
    - Objectives achieved most and least successfully
    - Training and development undertaken.

Time should be provided and utilised to complete the self-assessment, prior to the review interview. This should be completed as it assists you to organise your thoughts and focus on your achievements and areas for development. Without preparation, the interview may not achieve what you require. It is also particularly difficult to identify areas of weakness, examples, and then identify ways to develop improved performance in the area without adequate consideration.

Chastain (1980) suggested writing a memo to the appraiser prior to the appraisal. This would provide evidence of your achievements since the last review, future desires for your career, and some areas that you would like to discuss. Some of these areas may be covered in the self-assessment form used, however any opportunity to prepare the appraiser, and focus their mind on your strengths and achievements should be used especially if the IPR is linked to PRP.

## Stage 2

*Face-to-face interview*

- This interview should take as long as required to be able to cover all aspects of the IPR. It can last anywhere between 30 minutes and 2 hours.

- It is helpful to view the IPR interview as an opportunity to have positive quality time with your manager, where positive and negative feedback can be provided.

- An output of this interview is a report. This is discussed, agreed and signed by both parties. If you do not agree on the report the organisation should have a process in place to manage this. You should be made aware of the procedure during the organisation's IPR training. At the very least, the disagreement should be recorded (LRD, 1990)

- The form is retained by both parties, and objectives and personal development plan forwarded to human resources.

- It is not always a natural behaviour to objectively review your performance. You may find it hard to openly discuss your strengths or weaknesses. Again, it is advisable to attempt to predict the nature of the appraiser feedback in order that you are not surprised. Chastain (1980) comments that some women find it impossible to do this without crying. If this is something that you may do, develop a strategy to deal with it. Identify trigger situations, reflect on previous experiences and attempt to identify alternative ways to approach the situation. Chastain suggests that you may be able to become detached and analytical, or alternatively acknowledge the feedback, and suggest that you have some time to consider it, and arrange an alternative time to discuss. However, you should develop your own way of engaging with these situations.

- The interview should produce an objective setting element. Both you and the appraiser should have previously considered appropriate objectives for the forthcoming year. Your objectives should be able to demonstrate your contribution to the organisations overall goals. You will be able to identify likely objectives set by your manager/appraiser by reviewing the expectations of you at different levels. These would include:
    - The organisation's mission statement, values and business plan
    - The local department objectives
    - The managers' objectives

- The key result areas of your job description or job role
- There may also be other un-stated expectations of you and your role, which you should also capture.

## *Personal development plan*

- The actual interview should produce a personal development plan, which you both agree. The thinking and research you have undertaken in the preparation phase will inform you, and enable you to influence the direction of the development plan.

- Managers will always be more interested in development, which does not have a direct financial cost, and so always suggest a combination of ways of achieving development. Some of these may include:
  - Shadowing others who undertake roles similar to that which you are interested in for your next role.
  - Secondments to other departments, or acting up into a role vacated by sickness, holiday or maternity leave for example.
  - A request to take a lead role on a committee or group which may develop your profile within the organisation or expertise in a particular area, and which may utilise skills which you want to further enhance.

## *Rating or PRP*

- If appraisal is linked with PRP, the interview will also generate a performance rating. This will determine your performance related pay. Some criticise PRP as often it is a team-based award, but with an individual recipient. More commonly these days, the calculation involves an individual, department and an organisational performance rating.

## **Stage 3**

## *Mini review*

- This is held to follow up the IPR and may be held anywhere between 3 and 6 months later. It is helpful to undertake these mini reviews, as they can identify problem areas and generate development plans to overcome any shortfall. There should be no nasty surprises in the actual IPR, as feedback should be continuous.

## Conclusion

Legislation supports the espoused theory of equal pay and employment opportunities for women. However, women in the public sector earn 3–5% more than colleagues in the private sector, and women generally earn only 82% of the salary of their full-time male colleagues.

- The causes of the gender pay gap are varied and complex, however, they are not justifiable. By becoming aware of the causes, women can actively develop strategies to counter them.

- Every element of your performance will be useful to you when negotiating your salary. This includes:
    - The application form and documentation
    - Interview preparation, performance and follow-up
    - Job performance and appraisal.

- Aim for a win-win situation when negotiating a salary. Prepare in advance by rehearsing conversations, obtaining feedback and putting yourself in the situation of the employer to identify likely questions and obstacles. Postpone conversations about salary until you are prepared and ready to discuss it.

- Acknowledge that women discriminate against themselves by not making the most of, and openly acknowledging, their contribution to their success and the success of the organisation. Modesty will not get you that pay rise, promotion, or high PRP rating.

- Research the role and benchmark the likely salary range. Identify your acceptance threshold and pitch your salary 5–20% higher than the top of the salary range you have identified.

- Research salary progression mechanisms in the organisation and how they relate to your role. That is, IPR, automatic increments, collective bargaining or promotion. Negotiate a review date at the same time as your starting salary.

- Do not avoid appraisal. This is your opportunity to influence the direction of your role, objectives, personal development and rewards.

- Seek and accept any opportunity to be trained in the appraisal process used by your organisation prior to undertaking the review.

- Prepare for the IPR, including providing an evaluation of your past, current and future performance in advance of the review to promote your strengths. You should not be disadvantaged due to any absences.

- Review the outcome of the IPR, and dispute it if you do not agree with it, as documentation will be kept on your personal file.

- The appraisal interview can be an opportunity for you to become more focused, motivated and to improve your job satisfaction.

- Develop strategies in advance to deal with any anticipated negative feedback, and any negative emotional responses that you might experience.

- Ensure that you have access to a follow-up review to measure your performance against the baseline of your performance in the actual appraisal interview and implement any changes required at this time. Agree this date at your IPR interview.

## Notes

1. Harper, D. (2002) Balancing the Pay Scales, *People Management*, 10 January, p.17.

2. *Final Report to the Women and Equality Unit*, Anderson *et al.* (2001) p.1.

3. Swaffield, J. (2000) *Gender, Motivation, Experience and Wages* (London CEP).

4. Rosenthal, P. Guest, D., & Reccei, P. (1996) 'Gender differences in managers', Causal explanations for their work performance, *Journal of Occupational and Organisational Psychology*, Vol. 69, No. 2. pp.145–151.

5. Adapted from Redman *et al.* (2000).

6. Adapted from Redman *et al.* (2000).

## References

Anderson, T., Forth, J., Metcalf, H. & Kirby, S. (2001) *Final Report to the Women and Equality Unity*, Cabinet Office, September.

Benería, L. (1999) The enduring debate over unpaid labour, *International Labour Review*, Vol. 138, No.3.

Chastain, S. (1980) *Winning the Salary Game: Salary Negotiation for Women* (UK, John Wiley & Sons).

Giddins, G.E.B & Turner, J.E. (1995) Personnel appraisal, *British Journal of Healthcare Management*, Vol. 1, No. 2, pp.82–86.

Havard, B. (2001) *Performance Appraisals* (London, Kogan Page).

Harper, D. (2002) Balancing the Pay Scales, *People Management*, 10 January, p.17.

Jacobsen, J.P., Pearce, J.W. & Rosenbloom J.L. (1999) The effects of childbearing on married women's labour supply and earnings, *Journal of Human Resources*, Vol. 34, No. 3, Summer, pp.448–74.

Labour Research Department (LRD) (1990) *Performance Appraisal & Merit Pay*.

Pudney, S. & Shields, M.A. (1990) *Gender and Racial Discrimination in Pay and Promotion for NHS Nurses*, Discussion Paper No. 85, December.

Ka-ching Yan, F., Redman, T., Snape, E. & Thompson, D. (2000) Performance Appraisal in an NHS Hospital, *Human Resource Management Journal*, Vol. 10. No. 1, pp.48–62.

Walsh, J. (2000) Employers urged to mind the earnings gap, *People Management*, 16 March, p.14.

*Tips for Women at Work*

# Chapter 5
## *Personal Presentation*

**April Brown**

### Introduction

When I first emerged from obligatory uniforms and into 'ordinary' clothes, I have to admit that I got it 'wrong' on numerous occasions. I wore the wrong length skirts, wore dresses that were too bohemian for the workplace and because I felt I hadn't quite got my image right, I felt uncomfortable. I possessed only one suit that I perceived should only be used for interviews and not for everyday work wear. It wasn't until my second job where I was required to wear 'ordinary clothes' that I gradually understood the need for and began to discover my own style.

I have prepared this chapter for all women that may be embarking on a return to work outside of the home, or those like me a few years ago, who have the feeling that they haven't got it quite right and who are in need of a little guidance and advice. I admit that the world of clothing and fashion must be confusing if you are returning to work, or revamping your image, as the female fashion press is crammed with information all advising slightly different things. However, I don't profess to know it all, I am certainly not a fashion guru, but from my past experience and a keen eye for detail, my aim is to provide you with a helping hand. I am aware that not all corporate work environments require similar attire, for example in advertising and the media, the fashion has a tendency to be a little more relaxed, but I hope you will find that some elements of the chapter will be useful.

## Hair

- Regular professional maintenance is essential, don't be tempted to trim or colour your hair without professional assistance – the results could be disasterous.

- Conditioner can improve the appearance and manageability of hair.

- Remember to carry a small comb or brush in your handbag to keep your hair tidy during the day.

- If time is limited, speak to your hairdresser about low maintenance styles.

- Use hair accessories wisely and ensure that they project the image you want.

## Cosmetics

- Take advantage of the advice available at cosmetic counters in major department stores. Often the consultants will apply make-up for you and the cost is often reduced if items are subsequently purchased. Whilst you are with the consultant ask about your skin type as different skins will demand different care, which can affect the appearance of make-up.

- Once familiar with the skin care and make-up routine, it can be done quite quickly, i.e. under 15 minutes.

- Keep up-to-date, with seasonal colour changes even if only the lipstick is changed.

- For those women with darker skins, at last, there are a number of cosmetic houses that provide make-up which compliment the range of skin tones. These cosmetic companies tend to be found in large department stores in main cities, for example, London, Birmingham and Manchester.

- Discard mascara after 6 months as bacteria can develop and may cause eye infections.

- Refrain from sharing make-up with friends as this can encourage bacterial spread, which may lead to skin breakouts.

- In warm conditions, some lipsticks have a tendency to melt, so keep them in the office fridge during the day and the kitchen fridge when you are at home.

- You may require two different foundations during the year, as skin tones may change during the warm summer months.

## Clothes

Make an appointment with a fashion adviser. This service is increasingly available in department stores and often the advice is free of charge. The adviser will assess your requirements and then will be able to advise you on the following:

- What to wear.
- What colours are fashionable and more importantly what compliments your hair and skin tone.

If you have young children, or you just simply do not have the time to meander around the shops, then there is now an extensive range of home shopping alternatives, either via a home order catalogue or via the Internet. Many companies now offer speedy delivery. Shopping at home can provide many advantages:

- You can view the clothes in 'natural' light as opposed to 'shop' light.
- You can try on the clothes in your own time, without feeling rushed. Therefore, you may be less likely to make 'mistake' purchases.
- Deliveries and returns are via a courier and so make the process easier.

*Additional considerations:*

- Many suits are now washable and so reduce the need for a constant stream of clothes to be sent and collected from the dry cleaners.
- Trousers for women are more acceptable today.
- Skirt lengths vary, but again, look at what is available in the shops and catalogues and remember to ask for help from the shop assistants.
- Steer away from cardigans, although comfortable, they fail to project a sense of authority in the corporate world and should be left at home.
- Consider carefully the pattern of clothes, i.e. try not to mix stripes, spots and other patterns. It is safer to have a patterned suit and then a plain top or vice versa. If patterns are mixed, it can create quite a confusing look.

*Care for your clothes:*

- Store clothes correctly on hangers.
- Ensure that hemlines are intact and not worn or frayed.

*Tips for Women at Work*

- Iron and press clothes carefully.
- Observe the advice on the wash care label.
- Keep your wardrobes and cupboards tidy. In this way, you can see what additions and amendments are required. Also items can be easily chosen without the need for a daily chaotic search.

**Shoes and hosiery**

- Look carefully at what is available in shops and home shopping catalogues.
- Be careful not to wear heels that are too high. Heels can improve leg shape and of course provide additional height. However, if the heel is too high then this can adversely affect your posture.
- The code may change slightly during the summer months, but shoe colour should match the colour of your handbag or briefcase.
- Ensure that shoes are kept clean and well-healed.
- Always keep a spare pair of tights or stockings in your handbag in case 'ladders' occur.
- Wear tights or stockings that match and compliment the shoes and clothes that are being worn, i.e.:
    - Black suit, black or nearly black hosiery and black shoes.
    - Navy suit, navy or skin tone hosiery, navy shoes.
- During the summer months, then the choice not to wear tights and stockings is tempting. However, not all of us are blessed with naturally dark skin or an even skin tone. So take advantage of the range of self-tanning creams that are available to provide a little colour. Cosmetic tights can now be purchased; they have a fine denier and will even out the skin tone.
- If sandals are worn during the summer, then treat yourself to a pedicure each month or every two weeks if possible. Alternatively learn to carryout pedicures at home.
- Many of us commute into work that can involve quite considerable distances. Many American women now wear trainers during the journey to work and then put their 'day' shoes on when they reach the office, which is kinder for your feet.

# Personal Presentation

- Tights and stockings now have lycra incorporated into them and so they provide a better fit. Also, some hosiery has a slight sheen, which can add a touch of subtle glamour.

## Handbags

There are a range of methods for carrying one's personal affects these days and so here is some advice for you in order to make your choice:

- Carrying a bag in your hand is often preferable to shoulder bags as these can spoil the line of the clothes that are being worn and can exacerbate a poor posture.

- Again, black is the colour that is easy to manage and is easily sought.

- Detoxify your handbag each week and remove unwanted items and restore order. The unwanted items could be adding extra unnecessary weight.

- New technology such as laptop computers are very helpful, but unfortunately, accompanied with their wires can weigh in total up to 8kg. Therefore, it may be wise to use another new 'invention', the small trolley suitcase. These are ideal for transporting paperwork and laptops in a smart and trouble free manner. Many business people use them and they are no longer asked if they are going on holiday! A small suitcase is preferable to carrying numerous bags which can look like you are back packing rather than attending a meeting.

- Never re-use shop carrier bags to carry documents, invest in a briefcase which looks more professional.

## Jewellery

These are just a few of the golden rules that I have learned over the years from magazines and matriarchal figures in my life.

- Never mix gold and silver – decide which metal you want to wear. However, if you have a gold wedding or partnership ring on your hand then aim to keep the choice of metal consistent for that hand.

- If you have pierced ears, then make an effort and wear earrings. Double and multiple piercings would not achieve the professional image that is required.

- Keep large hooped and drop earrings for outside the work arena.

*Tips for Women at Work*

- Decide what you are going to wear and avoid wearing everything. As a guide:
    - Earrings, rings, bracelet
    - Earrings, necklace, rings.
- Avoid wearing ankle chains. Although they are pretty, again this is something that should be saved for after work.
- Purchase, simple, tidy jewellery.
- Good quality and reasonably priced costume jewellery is now readily available so updating one's look need not be an expensive exercise.
- Remember that jewellery should enhance a look, but should not dominate the scene – less is more.
- Pearl necklaces can look stylish on occasion, but wear with caution as they can have an ageing affect.

**Nails**

- Long nails for professional women are not practical and could be high maintenance which could pose a problem if you are pushed for time.
- Keep nails clean and neat.
- If nails fail to grow to a reasonable length, then there are acrylic options that can solve that problem.
- Moisturise hands at least three times a day.
- Either learn how to manicure your own nails or make frequent visits to a nail technician. Nail technicians have grown in popularity and can be found along most high streets and shopping centres and so the cost has reduced. Some companies can provide a manicure in less than 60 minutes and so can be undertaken during your lunch break.
- If a nail is broken or needs trimming, then file it with an emery board. Don't use a metal board or scissors as this can weaken the nail.

*If you decide to manicure your own nails then follow these basic tips:*

- Don't manicure your nails in a rush, it won't be successful.
- Remove old polish.
- Use a cuticle remover solution and push back and trim the cuticles.

- Shape the nail using an emery board.
- Buff the nails if you wish to remove fine ridges.
- Use a base coat, to ensure that the nail varnish adheres and to prevent staining of the nail itself.
- Use two–three coats of nail colour.
- Now use a top coat to protect the colour.
- If time is at a premium and you can't sit still for long then use a nail drying spray. This will ensure that the nails are hard to the touch within 5 minutes.
- Once a nail is chipped, remove the paint from all the nails and restart the process.
- As a general rule, nail varnish will only last 3 to 4 days before it needs to be redone.
- If you don't have the time or inclination to paint your nails, then just ensure that they are clean and neatly filed.
- If your nail bed is large or you have long nails, then darker colours can work well. If however, you have short nails or a small nail bed, then lighter colours are more appropriate

## Perfume

There are many fragrances on the market with more being launched each week. However, only certain perfumes will suit your skin chemistry. Spend time at the perfume counter, but be careful not to sample more than four in one day as your nose will become confused. It is important to have the perfume on your skin for at least 30 minutes and then smell it again to make sure that it suits you. Body heat can also slightly change the fragrance. As a general rule:

| | |
|---|---|
| Autumn/Winter/cold climates | Use more intense fragrances, musk, spicy, woody tones. |
| Spring/Summer/warm climates | Floral and fruity tones. |

After a while you will discover what fragrances best correlate to your mood and personality.

## Travel

Even with the advent of the digital age and express communications, international business travel may be part of your working life. If so, then some practical tips about how to make the most of your appearance whilst you are in transit.

I thought travelling light was an impossible concept to achieve. However, with practice and having been stung by excess baggage payments, here a few pointers to help you:

- Pack a combination of a matching suit, which may include jacket, trouser, skirt and dress. This may enable you to last 3 days in the same combination with a change of tops or blouses.

- Pack two pairs of shoes.

- Decant shampoo and lotions into small bottles.

- Save the free samples from magazines for travelling.

- Buy mini size versions of hairspray and shower gel.

- Instead of folding, roll tops to reduce creasing and avoid ironing.

- On arrival hang creased clothes in the bathroom, as the steam from the bath or shower will help to eliminate some of the creases.

- Take advantage of the hotel laundry facilitates to maintain your look.

- Pack a travel iron for increased convenience.

- If you are flying on a long haul route, you may wish to wear more comfortable clothes in-flight and then change towards the end of the flight if you are required to attend meetings as soon as you land.

- Remove make-up if you are flying for more than 6 hours. Keeping make-up on may dry out the skin and skin needs to be moisturised whilst flying due to the dry conditions in the cabin.

- Purchase a water spritz to maintain moisture on the face.

- Drink plenty of non-carbonated soft drinks to reduce the effects of dehydration and to improve the appearance the skin.

I hope this contribution has enabled you to gain a few tips and provided you with more confidence when you next hit the shops!

# Chapter 6
## Managing Home, Work and Time

**Andrée le May**

### Introduction

Managing time is one of the most essential and yet difficult elements of our lives to get right. This paradox has always puzzled me since on the face of it time management seems quite straightforward – after all we only have a finite amount of time so you'd think that it would be relatively easy to decide what to do with that time and simply use it in that way – that however is rarely the case! The trouble is that, because we all have different components in our lives – work, home and our lives outside both work and home, we are presented with many competing demands on that finite amount of time and this competition leads us into a constant juggling act.

As I write this I am wondering how good I really am at managing time – some would say superb since I usually do what I commit myself to on time, some would say hopeless since to 'deliver on time' I often borrow time from one part of my 'life' and lend it to another. A good example of that is today – as I write this paragraph it is six o'clock on a Thursday morning and I have taken the day off work to get my hair done, buy Christmas presents whilst the children are at school, collect cushions from a shop an hour's drive away and generally to relax before going to watch my daughters in two dance displays during the evening! At the moment the children are asleep, the dogs are also asleep having been walked, watered and fed – all is quiet, save the gentle sloshing of the washing machine, and I have grabbed an hour of writing so that I will meet the deadline (now too rapidly approaching) for this chapter. If I'd started writing 3 weeks ago, just before I moved house I could have had an extra hour's sleep today – but then I needed to use that time for packing boxes! I expect many of you are nodding your heads all too knowingly – some of you are thinking that sounds OK – she's worked out her priorities, bargained and juggled with time and made some sacrifices along the way – but generally that's fine because the jobs are getting done; others of you are thinking 'she's mad!' and are about to stop reading this chapter and rush out to buy one of those slim books containing handy hints for time management and send it to me! But seriously, the most important thing is, that crazy as it might seem to anyone other than myself, I have learnt to manage time in a way that best suits my life as it currently is, and perhaps that is the real secret of time management – getting a 'fit' between what you want and what you can (or have to) do. The trouble with that is that we aren't just managing our own time since the main demands on our time are made by other people and the ways in which they manage their time will impact greatly on our ability to use our own time effectively.

Time is undoubtedly an important resource to which we individually assign a particular value, for some it is the central element in the management of our lives – everything is always done on time, to time; whereas to others it is simply something that calmly passes by. One thing that is certain though is that time cannot be replaced or reversed (Adair, 1987). This chapter then is really about helping you to consider how you can get that best 'fit' between what you want to do, what is demanded of you and how much time you have to do it in. In order to try to do this I have chosen to identify key elements of successful time management and describe some exercises that you might find useful in helping you to become more aware of your time management strengths and weaknesses. But before we do that let's try to define time management.

## Defining time management

There are surprisingly few general definitions of time management – perhaps because it is obviously and simply about how we use time. There is, however, a general agreement that time management is about using time to our best advantage. In other words time management is not simply about getting a job done within a given time – it is about doing it well, with the appropriate amount of effort being spent and enjoying doing it and its ultimate outcome. In order to do this La Monica (1994) suggests, 'The time management process focuses on managing the self so that the ratio of effort to payoff is high'. When payoff outstrips effort we start to feel frustrated and pressured and we stop enjoying what we are doing even if we meet the deadlines set for us.

Some suggest that the focus of our use of time can be divided into components – for instance La Monica writes, within the context of management in general, about two categories of time – speciality time and managerial time. She describes speciality time as time which 'involves responsibilities which have to be accomplished alone' whereas managerial time 'involves some level of interaction between or among people' (p.283). This, although used by La Monica within a management framework, can help us to understand a fundamental component of time management – that some tasks are done by ourselves (and therefore are perhaps easier to arrange and time manage) whereas others are done with other people (and are therefore more complicated to arrange and time manage).

## Highlighting some of the key elements of successful time management

There are many books about time management and this section draws on some of these texts in order to highlight the key elements of successful time management. It should however not be read in isolation from some of the strategies that you have already devised to best manage your own time.

Good time management seems to focus around three important actions:

1. Identifying what to spend time on and how much time to spend on it.
2. Identifying and working with competing demands on time.
3. Evaluating how time has been used and considering how it could have been used more effectively.

Each of these, together with some strategies for helping you to work with time, is discussed as follows.

## Identifying what to spend time on and how much time to spend on it

If time management is about getting a job done well within a specified time, devoting an appropriate level of effort to that job and enjoying doing it then the first element of successful time management must be to decide what to spend time on. In my experience this requires a degree of ruthlessness coupled with the ability to negotiate not only with others but also with yourself about how you spend time, as well as the ability to say no without feeling guilty.

In order to do this it is important to do a bit of future gazing. Adair suggests planning long-, middle- and short-term goals as an important facet of deciding what to spend time on. Knowing what you want to achieve – and of course doing that from a 'whole life perspective' so that you can think about the ways in which each of the different goals impact on each other – is, however, not as easy as it sounds. Although each of us probably has some long-term goals that we want to achieve it is hard to decide on a timeframe for achieving these since there are so many expected and unexpected things that might get in the way. But this shouldn't deter you from trying to think of the most important things for you to achieve in every facet of your life and then working out when you want to do this by. Once you have decided on these long-term goals the next thing is to work backwards and see what needs to be done towards reaching these goals and allocate times to each of them. Try to do this now using the template for looking ahead in Box 1 as a way of ordering your thinking.

---

**Goal to aim for.**

**Time by which goal needs to be achieved.**

---

**Box 1.** Template for looking ahead.

Once you have done this and decided to stick with these goals you need to ruthlessly consider whether or not to do anything that isn't important to these outcomes and review them regularly to check if they are still feasible and desirable. In reality, however, this is of course easier said than done but at least it's somewhere to start from and to refer to periodically when you feel that you are deviating from the route that you set out on.

## Identifying and working with competing demands on time

Looking into the future may also have led you to identify things in your day-to-day life which compete with each other and therefore stop you managing time as effectively as you could – some things may be described as positive consumers of time (things you have to do and/or enjoy) whereas others are time wasters and do not have to be done – recognising which is which will help you with your daily time management.

Whilst our ability to reach long-term goals is always in the back of our minds we are more likely to be worried by the day-to-day management of time – given that lack of time is often one of the things that is highlighted as causing stress and anxiety. In relation to day-to-day time management Adair has proposed some useful tips for managing time at work that could equally be applied to other areas of life. He reminds us of the value of planning the day through drawing up a daily list of:

- What you have to do (therefore identifying the things which conflict in that list).
- What you will do with any free time (either planned or unplanned, for example, through the cancellation of meetings).

Drawing up these lists is fairly straightforward, the tricky bit is to set time limits for each of the jobs and then to prioritise them into those that have to be done today and those which can wait (and thereby become the ones that have to be done tomorrow!). One way to prioritise is to start with jobs that will have benefit to you (or others) but can be completed quickly; another useful tip is to clutch together similar jobs (e.g. making telephone calls or answering emails). The other trick is to delegate work to others – so time thinking about how this can be done is time well spent. Adair suggests that this list making helps us to use time effectively but he also warns against turning into a 'time fanatic' (p.63) who is so smug about her management of time that she drives others (perhaps less able at time management) to distraction by spreading handy tips on using time to best effect!

In addition to the use of lists to allow us to make the best possible use of time Adair suggests that we focus on the quality of time as well as the quantity of time. To help to do this you need to identify the times of day when you feel at your best and those when you are at your worst. You are probably thinking that this task is easy – but you might be surprised at how poorly you know yourself – so ask someone you work with to help you. Once you have identified your good times keep the difficult jobs for then.

At the end of each day check back over your list, review the things that you have done 'to time' and those which you have been unable to achieve and why. This will help you identify competing priorities and unrealistic allocations of time to various tasks – after that start to think about tomorrow's list.

List keeping is, for me, a great way to keep a check on what I'm doing and still have to do but it is easy to leave out several important features of living when you draw up a list focusing on completing tasks, so in addition to the content of your list, remember to allow enough time for:

- Rest
- Relaxation
- Thinking.

## Evaluating how time has been used and considering how it could be used more effectively

Although as Adair rightly says you cannot manage time that is past it is always worth evaluating how well you have used your time. One way to do that is to identify critical incidents during which you have either managed time well or badly and think through how the good bits of your time management could be transferred to other instances and the poorer bits improved upon. Consider yesterday and use the template in Box 2 to help you identify critical incidents and think about them in relation to your personal management of time.

---

Critical incident(s).

Examples of good time management and related actions.

Examples of poor time management and related actions.

---

**Box 2.** Thinking about how I manage time.

## Factors which impact on our ability to manage time well

Adair highlights several common time problems – at the top of his list is ourselves because we are essentially time wasters! He suggests that we have developed highly skilled strategies for putting things off, failing to delegate things to others, ineffectively managing other people and not really knowing what we, ourselves, are meant to be doing. Being aware of this is an essential element in good time management.

Within the workplace there are many factors which impact on our ability to manage time well – they may be linked to us or to others. Three of the main ones are detailed below:

1. The increased use of email to communicate with people has meant that we spend a long time reading and answering a mountain of emails instead of memoranda. Interestingly, most of us give this process high priority because our email correspondents expect almost instantaneous answers – long gone are the delays associated with postage – and the resultant feeling that there was time to think before replying! Although email has reduced the mountain of paperwork there are some tips that used to be applied to paperwork which are just as useful to apply to electronic communication – these Adair refers to as classifying mail (electronic or in paper form) for action, information, reading or binning (either electronically through deletion or literally in the waste-paper bin). He advises also having a way of identifying information that you want to leave alone for a bit – either to think through or cool off about – and having a strategy for doing this.

2. Meetings are often viewed as time wasting especially when they start late or over-run or you feel that you are not the right person to contribute to the area being considered. Adair describes strategies for managing meetings effectively – suggesting that there are five types of meeting – and that each should be used appropriately to ensure your own and other's time management is not impeded by inefficiency.

    a. A briefing meeting is where instruction surrounding the undertaking of a task are given.
    b. An advisory meeting on the other hand is essentially about exchanging ideas and information.
    c. A council meeting is characterised by decision-making based on consensus with associated accountability.
    d. A committee meeting is one in which representatives from particular groups meet to make decisions about common concerns.
    e. A negotiating meeting is one in which representatives of different interests get together to resolve differences and identify a way forward.

Knowing the sort of meeting that you are attending or facilitating means that you can lay down ground-rules and manage allocated time appropriately. Adair also suggests always asking if a meeting is necessary to call or to attend and reviewing each meeting's usefulness regularly.

Delegating to others – or managing people is an important element of managing one's own time and much emphasis is placed on this by Adair. However, it is also important to actively acknowledge that delegation will impact on other's ability to manage time as well.

## Conclusion

Managing time is an essential element of all of our lives. In order to do this well we have to think about our priorities in life, how these impact on or compete with each other, and in relation to these and other people's priorities, plan how to manage the time available to us most effectively to suit our needs and lifestyle.

## References

Adair, J. (1987) *How to manage your time* (Guildford, Talbot Adair).

La Monica, E. (1994) *Management in health care* (Basingstoke, Macmillan).

# Chapter 7
## *What about the Kids?*

### Sue Harrop and Sue Miller

### Introduction
One of the most significant issues for many women wanting to return to paid work after having a family is the organisation of their children's care. While there will inevitably be some additional 'juggling' to do when trying to balance the roles of mother with employee, reliable, good quality, accessible and affordable childcare is recognised as being one of the most important factors in allowing women to return to work.

Until fairly recently, finding suitable childcare to allow women to work had been left entirely to families to sort out. However, in 1998 the current Labour government published the document 'Meeting the Childcare Challenge'. In the forward to this document, Tony Blair wrote:

> *'We also want to ensure that families have access to good quality childcare. This matters to us all. To our children who deserve the best start in life. Good quality childcare – whether from parents, informal or professional carers – is vital to them growing up happy and secure in themselves, socially confident and able to benefit from education. To the many parents – especially mothers – who are unable to take up a job, education or training opportunities because childcare isn't available. To businesses, who suffer when skilled and talented people are unable to take up work.'*

The government subsequently produced a national strategy designed to address the issue of childcare and to create affordable and accessible childcare for over one million children by 2004. The strategy recognised that people needed help and support to get appropriate childcare. This childcare needed to be flexible, inclusive, able to respond to all children's needs, respectful of special needs and cultural diversity. Childcare was viewed as directly related to parents', and particularly mothers', ability to get to work.

In addition, the government introduced Working Family Tax Credit and Childcare Credit as a means to support families on lower incomes to be able to afford childcare and made it the responsibility of employers to help employees to make application for these through the Inland Revenue.

As a result of this and other government initiatives, there has been a growth in the amount and type of childcare available, although it is recognised that having choice in childcare still depends on where people live, their income and employment status.

## How do I feel about involving someone else in the care and education of my child?

There have been huge changes in society's views of what constitutes good mothering over the past hundred years. While women have always worked outside the home, out of necessity, nowadays many women choose to work for other reasons. Views about whether this is right or wrong have developed and been challenged by the practice of individuals and the various evidence of the impact having a working mother has on children's development.

The notion that women have the right to paid employment contrasts strongly with a view that going out to work, and particularly following a career, is somehow an indication of selfishness and irresponsibility on the part of women. This has led to concerns that the pendulum may have swung too far the other way so that it may now be frowned upon in some quarters for a woman, particularly one who has been well-educated and trained, to stay at home and be a full-time parent.

Whatever your views on this, it is important that you come to your own decision about how you and your family want to live your lives and think through carefully the various options. What suits one family may not suit another and if you feel that you are simply doing what is expected of you and not what you believe in, it is quite likely that you will not be comfortable with your choices.

It is important to know what you feel and to have the opportunity to really think about what you want to do, what you can afford to do and why you are doing it. How do you feel about involving someone else in bringing up your child? What are you going to work for? Money? Fulfilment? To maintain your identity? Status? Company? All of these?

It's probably worth considering before discussing childcare the extent to which you could achieve each of these either by not working, by working part-time, or by working full-time.

**What do the people closest to me feel about it?**
You are going to need the support of at least one or two of the following people: your partner, your family and your friends. Their attitude towards your decision will be very significant not only in terms of how you feel about them, but also how you feel about yourself. If they are negative about the decisions you take it is quite possible that you will have these undermined.

We know that previous experience can have a considerable influence on our values and beliefs about childcare. Coming from a family where the women have always had paid employment can bring as much of a pressure to conform to this model as one where mothers have stayed at home.

Whatever you decide to do, it can be very helpful to rehearse and try to understand with your nearest and dearest the implications of not having you available for childcare duties. This can be particularly an issue if you want to return to work when your family has grown accustomed to you being at home. You will all need to talk about what the impact will be on the everyday domestic help you need to organise as a family. Some women consider what jobs they currently do that they could contract out either to other family members or to a paid worker. It can help to think through how other members of the family may need to alter their days, ways of working, their view of their role in the childcare scenario and the family. Think about sorting out ground rules such as who is doing what tasks in the home and considering what the impact of you working out of the home might be on the time and energy you will have left to be available to your family in it. Remember through this that your family may be very proud of the fact that you have a paid role outside of the home as well as the role you have in it.

## How will I know/what will I do if it's not working out?

Whatever childcare arrangements you make, there is inevitably going to be some additional juggling involved in your family life and this can create stress. Taking regular health checks on yourself, your child and the rest of your family is crucial. It's important to have time for you. This will be a benefit not just for you, but for your family too. Listen to your children and listen to yourself.

Research has shown that worryingly high numbers of working mothers have no personal time that they can describe as being strictly for themselves. They may not give themselves permission even to have a medical appointment during the day.

If you find you are unhappy with the way your work-life balance is going, perhaps you are missing the children or do not enjoy feeling rushed or as if you are doing nothing well. Perhaps the situation is leaving you feeling less than comfortable about your performance as a parent, as a colleague, as a friend, as a partner. For many working women it is their friendships that they find suffer or their hobbies and their capacity for fun that reduce when they work. This can be very counterproductive, both for your emotional well-being and that of your family.

Trust your feelings. If you are feeling unhappy, this does not have to be a reflection of all areas of your life. Try to trace these feelings back to find their source and achieve a work-life balance that suits you.

## What choices do I have?

If you still want to go ahead with finding childcare while you work, there are a number of choices

We are talking here not about crèche settings that parents typically use for short periods when they are doing an activity themselves such as shopping or sport, nor about playgroups or school nurseries run by education authorities which children typically attend for 2 hours a day (although remember that some playgroups can now offer sessional childcare of up to 4 hours).

These sorts of services would not be described as full-day care and generally they do not provide enough cover on their own for working mothers. They may incorporate these services as a part of what they use but 'wrap them round' with other support.

Although also generally not for more than 2 or 3 hours a day, we have included Out-of-school Clubs here because they cater for older children so may in fact be the main care provider after the school day.

Bear in mind that you have an increasing right to ask at your own work interviews about family friendly approaches. Does your employer have childcare facilities, flexi-time or home working?

And remember, it's not just you that makes this decision, it's your partner and your child. They all need to be involved. You all need to be happy.

The choices you have for full-day care are as follows:

- Unregistered care
- Care in your own home
- Care in someone else's home
- Care in a group setting
- Out-of-school care.

## Unregistered care – *the options*

### *Family member*

Could be one of a number of different people: grandparents, sister, brother, member of your extended family. They will typically live quite close to you.

### *Friend*

Again, they will usually live nearby and will probably have their own children that they look after and that your child knows and are therefore available at home. Some parents fit care by a friend around registered care such as a childminder, for example having a friend collect your child from school, but dropping your child off at a childminder who will look after your child until you get home from work. If this care takes place in your home or theirs, and there is no payment involved, then this is an entirely private arrangement and there is no registration necessary.

### *How do I find out what's available?*

You are going to know these people and will have seen them with their own children or with yours.

### *How do I know if it's a good quality service?*

You will have a feeling that this person has a similar set of values and beliefs, and way of working to you and that you and your children are happy with them. You know they like your child. You have observed them with their own children and yours. Trust your feelings and take note of how your child gets on with this person.

### *How much will it cost?*

It could be that there is no cost, but experience suggests that you really have to speak completely honestly about this and make sure that if this family member or friend wants payment they can tell you.

If they get paid in their own home or yours and are on any benefit or pension then they are breaking the law. They are not even supposed to receive 'in kind' payment such as gifts or flowers. Other registered carers may learn of such arrangements and you or your family member or friend could be reported to the authorities for receiving illegal payments.

### *Positives*

- You know the person and have confidence in them.
- Can be very cheap.
- Can constantly renegotiate childcare needs if you are going to be late or work different times or are going on holiday.
- Generally family members are happier to look after an ill child than paid carers might be.
- May be a fulfilling role for other members of the family, for example, recently retired and still young at heart grandparents.

### *Negatives*

- Not everyone has this option.
- Can lead to tensions and even destroy previous good relations if resentments build up.
- You need to be sure that this person does not resent you going out to work while they are at home.
- Payment can be a contentious issue and difficult to discuss with someone who is a family member or friend.

- Can be difficult to lay down your expectations with a family member. They may discipline your child the way they did you, but you may not necessarily want this to happen to your child.

- You lose some of your separateness from your parents if they get too involved with your children.

- People get older and grandparents may just not have the energy to look after the child.

*What do parents say?*

Jenny: 'Financially it's been the best solution for me, but it's not straightforward because although we've got the same values, we still have to negotiate lots of things.'

*What do children say?*

Billie (3 years old): 'I like going to my Gran's because she gives me treats.'

*Verdict*

Good solution if you're on a tight budget, and you've got family or friends nearby, but requires lots of honesty and openness to avoid resentment.

**In your own home** – *the options*

*Au pair*

An au pair is typically a young person, more often than not a female, who wants to come to another country to learn a language and is prepared to work for their keep by caring for the children of the host family. They will expect to live in your home, receive board and keep and a small allowance. In return, they can be expected to carry out some basic childcare duties and to oversee the care of your children while you are at work. Often they will not have childcare qualifications, but may have some informal general babysitting experience.

*Nanny*

Nannies are qualified childcare workers who may live with you and your family or may travel to work from their own homes. You can expect them to have the capacity to undertake the full range of childcare and educational roles, particularly with young children and babies.

### How do I find out what's available?

There are a number of agencies that advertise widely in yellow pages or through your local authority's Children's Information Service (CIS). Many childcare magazines will carry adverts for nannies and au pairs as will local colleges that offer childcare courses.

### How do I know if it's a good quality service?

Although there are moves to develop a voluntary Code of Practice for recruiting agencies, this is currently the least well-regulated form of paid childcare. You should ask for references, a full employment history and carry out an interview, but none of these approaches is foolproof.

References have their limitations. It's a good idea to ask if you can phone up and talk to someone who the person has worked for in the past. With au pairs you are probably going to have an unqualified, inexperienced woman who may at best have had some babysitting experience. They may have good social skills and be resourceful, but you cannot expect them necessarily to know a great deal about children. Once they are in post, you may want to spend some time at home with the au pair to reassure yourself about her capabilities. Watch how your children react and if appropriate, ask them how they feel about the person caring for them. You should have a contract that may be drawn up through an agency to clarify roles and responsibilities.

Nannies and au pairs can find life in someone else's home quite stressful. If they are living at a distance from their normal home base, you may have to take some responsibility for developing their social networks.

### How much will it cost?

If the person is living in your home, you can expect to pay tax and national insurance because you are employing them. You also have to pay for their food.

For prices contact your local nanny agencies through yellow pages to get a feel for fees. If you want to have the person checked for criminal records or social service checks you would have to pay for this.

### Positives

- Your child is familiar with their own toys and surroundings.
- You can leave a child in bed if you need to go to work very early.
- The nanny or au pair may be able to do household jobs.

- Your child plays with and gets to know local children, thus making own networks.
- Can look after children of different ages.
- Could have consistency throughout childhood if nanny stays with your family for years.
- If you move house, a nanny might move with you.

**Negatives**

- Have to share personal home space with a stranger.
- House will be untidy, children will be there all day.
- Other people's children may come into your home while you are at work.
- May be a short-term contract, cannot depend on it being consistent. Au pairs will definitely be expected to be a short-term temporary arrangement.
- Need to be careful not to ask too much of them and to spoil the relationship.
- May have to teach childcare skills if young/inexperienced in childcare.
- You are employing them so the responsibility of being an employer falls to you. You have to sort out National Insurance, holidays, etc.
- You may be responsible for finding a network of support for the person.

**What do parents say?**

Annie: 'My hours are so irregular and I often have to work very late, way past the hours a nursery would be open. With two children under 5 an au pair or nanny were really the only options as it meant that I could leave the children asleep if I had an early call, or that they'd be able to be put to bed at a reasonable time if I was late. The house isn't that big and you do lose some privacy and it does feel odd to come home sometimes to a house full of children you don't know that have been invited in, which can happen with a nanny who has friends that are also nannies. But at least with an au-pair it means we've always got a babysitter and that's eased things for us if we need some time to ourselves.'

**What do children say?**

Finlay (4 years old): 'I like Anna. She plays with me and makes me my lunch.'

*Verdict*

Good option if your hours are irregular, but be prepared to share your space and perhaps have to invest in training.

## In someone else's home – *the options*

*Childminder*

Childminders are self-employed people, generally women though sometimes men, who care for children in their own homes. They have to be registered with OFSTED (Office for Standards in Education), which is now responsible for registration, inspection and quality assurance. The CIS in your local authority will be able to supply you with a list of names and details for childminders in your area. Strict regulations govern how many children they can take and at what ages. Childminders are inspected and have to meet certain standards of care and safety in their homes, often more than you would expect in a private house. Childminders often have their own children at home too and are doing minding as a way of making some extra money while at home. They will generally take children from birth and may also have some children in their care who they just collect from school and in this way they act as an after school service.

Childminders are now being encouraged to adopt a more educational approach to their care role, and in some areas childminder networks have been set up to facilitate sharing of equipment but also so that if one of the network is ill another member can cover for her and still take your child. Some networks can deliver early years education to OFSTED standards.

Childminders and parents are expected to draw up a contract between themselves, which sets down the expectations and arrangements on both sides. Experience suggests that time spent getting this right reduces tensions and misunderstandings later.

*How do I find out what's available?*

Each local authority will have a CIS with a list of all the registered childminders in their area and they can very often say who has availability and from which schools if any they can collect children.

### *How do I know whether it's a good quality service?*

Often word of mouth is a good way of hearing about what a childminder is like. If they are popular and well liked and respected by other parents is this because they are a good service? You can ask to see the inspection reports, which OFSTED produces, on each childminder that they register. Childminders are now inspected once a year. This visit involves an inspection of the house and a consideration of whether they are a fit person to care for children. They will have been formally checked by the police and social services for any recorded offences as would other people over 16 who live in the childminder's home.

They are expected to keep records of accidents and of children's attendance and also of any medical treatment they have had to administer while your child was in their care.

You will want to know whether their home is a child friendly environment. You have to go on your own gut reaction to this, but look at the quality of the environment, the play space available, the toys, whether they take the children on outings. Now childminders can take up to 10 books out from a local library and many local authorities have toy libraries that can lend toys suitable for children with special needs. There is also training available for childminders. Some areas have childminder networks. These allow groups of childminders to meet, the children they mind to play together as well as providing opportunities for cover if your childminder is ill, as your child may be able to go to another minder in the network that they have met and know. A childminder network will have a quality assurance kite mark.

### *How much will it cost?*

Costs vary, depending on where you live. Individual arrangements are made with the parent if they wish the childminder to provide food, in which case the parent would be charged, or if the parent supplies this and the childminder just prepares it. Charges would also reflect whether the childminder or the parent supplies nappies. If this is the only child your childminder intends to care for and there are some changes that need to be made to the house to fulfil the conditions of registration, you may need to talk about who pays for this.

Everyone is now entitled to the minimum wage so you must pay this or you will be breaking the law. Most childminders do not earn enough to have to pay National Insurance or pensions.

Think about things like car seats, cots and buggies. Petrol costs, checking driving license and car seats are all important if you are asking the childminder to take your child in a car. New childminders can apply for a start up grant from the local Early Years Development and Childcare Partnership (EYDCP), but after that they need to find out what services are available. You may have to take responsibility to ensure they have safety equipment like cooker guards.

Many childminders will charge a retainer of half their fee over the child's holiday, though separate arrangements would need to be made by you to cover the childminder's holidays and any sick pay.

The National Childminding Association (NCMA) is the national organisation for childminders that sets standards for childminding and advises government about policies relating to them.

*Positives*

- Child becomes part of a new family.
- Can be relatively cheap.
- Relaxed and informal – more like home.
- Opportunity to develop a close relationship between child, parent and childminder.
- Can look after a range of ages from same family.
- Child can stay with a family for a long time.
- Usually local so can pick up from school.
- Newly registered childminders must, since the introduction of the childcare strategy, have a basic training as part of their registration and have access to further training.

*Negatives*

- Have to take child to and from childminder's home.
- Difficulties if the childminder is ill and cannot care for your child.
- The unstructured informality may not suit parents who want something more 'educational'.
- Generally not formally qualified, but experienced as parents.

- Childminders tend to work alone so you might feel that your child would be quite isolated.
- Your children may not necessarily get on with the childminder's own family or other children that attend.
- Childminders work alone and the regulation of childminders is relatively light touch. You have to make a personal judgement about how the person will behave when you are not around.
- One person becomes the main carer after you.
- For first time parents, having your child making such a close relationship with one other person outside the family could lead to feelings of jealousy and inadequacy.

### *What do parents say?*
Sue: 'I looked long and hard for a childminder I really felt I could trust. I felt comfortable with Lucy instantly. In fact, Kate now has two families, and regards Lucy's children as surrogate brothers and sister.'

### *What do children say?*
Kate (9 years old): 'I really love Lucy's house. It's fun because she's got Daisy who is my age and I can play with her.'

### *Verdict*
Works well if there is a professional level of relationship between the parent and the childminder and trust and respect on both sides for the contribution each is making to the child's care. Can go wrong if ground rules are not established at the beginning and regularly reviewed.

## **Group settings** – *the options*

### *Full-day care*
Can be run privately, on a voluntary basis or by a local authority. Should be open every day, and take children from between 6 weeks and 5 years of age. Opening hours can be from around 7.30 a.m. till 6.00 p.m. There are some moves to have settings open for longer and over weekends in certain parts of the country. Generally able to offer full- or part-time places. Caters fully for needs such as meals and sleep.

Staff generally hold a childcare qualification. There will be a range of activities, often with outdoor play and they may take children to activities.

Some have particular early childhood philosophies, for example, Montessori or Highscope and policies relating to areas such as equal opportunities and special needs.

Some large employers run their own childcare nurseries for staff, though not many, and this is something that the government would like to see expand. Some employers find a local nursery and pay to keep some places open there on a regular basis for their staff.

## *How do I find out what's available?*

Information about group day care settings is available through the CIS, yellow pages or by word of mouth.

## *How do I know whether it's a good quality service?*

You have to decide what you think a good setting needs to have and then look for that. Trust your own feelings. In general though, it should be registered through OFSTED and this will mean that, like childminders, it is regularly inspected. Ask to see the OFSTED report, which will be available in the setting itself or over the web.

When visiting, take your child with you and see how they react. Ask yourself:

- Will your child be safe?
- Will they be happy?
- Will they have consistency – what's staff turnover like?
- Will the setting reflect the society they live in?
- Will they be able to stay there for a long time because it has after school provision?
- Will it provide early years education? If it does there will be a reduction in your fees because the setting will get a grant from government to cover this.
- Does it have extras like music, language and dance?
- Is there evidence of staff training and qualifications via certificates, etc. on display?

- Does it have a key worker system?
- Do the children have visits and trips, for example, to the local library? What are the arrangements for these?

*How much will it cost?*

This depends on the area, though normally fees are per day. Cost will depend on the number of sessions and the age of your child and in general fees are higher for babies where the ratio of adults to children has to be the greatest. The CIS will be able to give you an indication of fees in your area and what these fees cover in the way of extras such as food and nappies. Some people will get reductions in fees because of their personal circumstances or means, or because they have more than one child attending.

*Positives*

- Stepping stone to school: children get used to being in a group.
- Qualified staff.
- Long opening hours.
- Cover for staff illnesses possible.
- Number of adults involved so do not have to rely on one person.
- Can see you through all of your child's pre-school childcare needs.
- Some actually will let you do a mix and match with a local education setting so your child does not 'miss out' on an educational place.
- You may feel more reassured that in these settings there are more checks and balances of care possible.
- Quality assurance schemes exist for settings and you can ask if the setting has any 'kite marks'.

*Negatives*

- Catering for the needs of a group means that it is more likely to have routines, for example, set times for meals, outings and sleep times. This can feel a less flexible arrangement than a home setting.
- This can effect the settings capacity to fit in with the individual child's rhythms.

- Private settings are businesses that have to make a profit and this will require the owner to balance paying for training, qualified staff and resources against the demands of a viable business.
- Staff work shifts and different children may attend at different times. Your child may not always see the same children or adults each session.
- For some children, going to the same place for several years can feel institutionalising.
- Your child may mix only with children of their own age because the setting is organised like this.
- Typically more expensive than other forms of day care.

*What do parents say?*

Claire: 'I felt I could trust my child's key worker and be reassured that my child is safe because there are lots of checks and balances. I could always rely on the nursery to be there.'

*What do children say?*

Thomas (4 years old): 'I like all the toys and Kelly's my special worker.'

*Verdict*

For people that work long hours and in inflexible and demanding jobs, this provides reliable long-term group care for preschool children. You can choose whether it's near where you work or where you live.

## Out-of-school care – *the options*

*Out-of-school clubs*

This is childcare for a child that is wrapped around the normal school day. It can be before school, after school, breakfast time and holiday play schemes.

It provides something different from school; a place children can play, do activities or homework and chill out. Parents have to book their child in, and pay on a sessional basis.

### How do I find out what's available?

The CIS in each local authority will have lists of available registered out-of-school care. They would know if there is a pick up service that will transport a child from a school that does not have out-of-school care to one that does.

Asking at your local school or playgroup or nursery will also tell you if they offer any hours over and above their core time.

### How do I know whether it's a good quality service?

You need to visit when the setting is operating. When visiting consider whether the setting will be able to provide for the needs of your children that they are likely to have at the time they are there.

Settings have to be registered through OFSTED if caring for children under 8 years of age and you can ask to see the OFSTED reports. Ask if staff are qualified, particularly in playwork and that the activities are appropriate for the age and the time of the day they are looking after children. Does it fit the children's natural rhythm? Can they relax if it's after school? If it's breakfast time, is it a chance for them to wake up properly? Does it offer an environment if they need to do homework that's appropriate? Are there computer facilities if they need them?

Will your child feel comfortable with the other children and be able to do what they want to do? Will your children be picked up and then brought to the setting? Will they get the sort of meal that they need? Will they be able to cope with the additional time they will be away from home?

If you are considering holiday play schemes ask whether they are offering a variety of appropriate activities that will keep children stimulated and happy all day. Is it a safe environment? Are they checking who comes in and out and who has a legitimate reason for being there? Are there appropriate arrangements for children's safety when they are taken out of the setting? Are risks properly assessed and responded to with older children? Have they got a quality assurance kite mark?

### How much will it cost?

These clubs are paid for on a sessional basis. Costs will depend on the age of the children and the length of time they are there

*Positives*
- Can be relatively cheap.
- Local.
- Very often children will be with their friends from school.
- Siblings can be looked after together.
- Can have play opportunities and visits you cannot give them.
- May have a homework club where they could get support with schoolwork.
- Flexible.
- Lengthens the time that you can stay at work or start work in the morning or over holidays.

*Negatives*
- Can make it a long day for young children.
- Keeps child away from their home-based activities.
- Not a home environment and children do get a longer period away from home.
- Can be problematic for older children who feel they could cope with being more independent and having more of a say about how they spend their leisure time.

*What do parents say?*

Jackie: 'I can pick Hannah up from the school and know that she's been looked after safely.'

*What do children say?*

Hannah (10 years old): 'It means I'm safe out of school. It's fun and there's lots of people you can play with. My mum can stay at work extra hours until she feels she needs to come and pick my sister and me up.'

*Verdict*

Good option particularly if you are on a tight budget. Out-of-school care is becoming easier to find in local areas as a result of government support.

### Who can I talk to for advice? Where do I go from here?

Apart from friends and family, some of whom may have vested interests and certainly their own perspectives on what children need, there are a number of organisations and websites you can visit:

Children's Information Service
www.childcare-info.co.uk

Kids Club Network
www.kidsclub.co.uk

National Childminding Association
www.ncma.org,uk

NDNA
www.ndna.org.uk

Need a Nanny?
www.dfes.gov.uk/nanny

Choosing a Childminder
www.childcare-info.co.uk/childcare/childmndr

What is an Out-of-School Club?
www.tameside.gov.uk

Daycare Trust
www.daycare trust.org.uk

Office of Standards in Education
www.dfes.gov.uk

Yellow pages

*Tips for Women at Work*

# Chapter 8
## Dealing with the Unexpected, Stress and Bullies

**Catherine Gaskell**

### Introduction

Being the target of bullying in the workplace and the subsequent stress associated with this can have a major impact on the well-being and health of working women. This chapter explores bullying behaviours in the workplace and gives practical advice on how to cope if you are being bullied. It uses anecdotal experiences of women who were targets in their workplaces and it includes theirs and others top tips for surviving the experience. The chapter concludes with 25 tried and tested stress busting antidotes and a list of helpful websites and reading for further advice support and information.

Many of the facts in this chapter can be attributed to examples and experiences on the UK National Bullying Advice line:

- Definitions of bullying
- Bullying behaviours
- Why are you being bullied?
- Who is getting bullied?
- Three women's stories
- Surviving the bullying experience

- 25 best stress-busting tips
- References, websites and further reading.

## Definition of bullying at work – taken from *Bullying at Work* by Tim Field (1999)

Bullying occurs when one person, typically (but not necessarily) in a position of power, authority, trust, responsibility, management, etc. feels threatened by another person, who is usually (but not always) a subordinate who is displaying qualities of ability, popularity, knowledge, skill, strength, drive, determination, tenacity, success, etc. The bullies have conditioned themselves to believe that they can never have these qualities, which they readily see in others.

The definition used by Manufacturing Science and Finance Union (MSF) is, 'Persistent, offensive, abusive, intimidating, malicious or insulting behaviour, abuse of power or unfair penal sanctions which makes the recipient feel upset, threatened, humiliated or vulnerable, which undermines their self-confidence and which may cause them to suffer stress.'

NASUWT (Career Teachers Organisation) define it as: 'The unjust exercise of power of one individual over another by the use of means intended to humiliate, frighten, denigrate or injure the victim.'

The Bully-online website defines bullying as 'behaviour which consistently undermines another's confidence, reducing feelings of self-worth and self-esteem.' Whatever definition of bullying you choose, it is a process where an individual in the workplace is systematically undermined, discriminated against, and treated in a way that hinders their delivery of work objectives.

Most people say they know when they are being bullied though recognition may not always occur at the time of the incident.

Descriptions of 'bullying behaviours' include:

- Constant or destructive criticism
- Marginalisation – being left out of decision-making
- Humiliation – in front of peers or junior staff
- Being given the silent treatment
- Excessive monitoring of performance and outputs
- Being starved of resources often hand-in-hand with being overworked

- Work being increased or removed
- Being isolated and excluded from the inner circle/decision-making
- Ridicule/or ideas and success stolen
- Unrealistic goals or deadlines being set.

This list is not exhaustive. Bullies can use and find a range of these and other behaviours to intimidate, belittle and destroy the confidence of their targets. Bullies are often described as being behaviourally immature, rigidly short-term in their outlook and constantly interfering, dictating and controlling. People who bully do so to avoid facing up to and dealing with their inadequacies. Other bullying tactics include using sarcasm, insults and personal comments, ridiculing ideas and managing performance in a negative and punitive way, controlling and dominating the target with threats of sanctions or the loss of their employment. Bullies also may work in pairs or groups and can thrive in certain environments.

**Symptoms of bullying – in the workforce**

Bullying which occurs over a prolonged period of time can have a number of effects on your life. Like the effects of stress it can have psychological effects on your confidence and as well as physical effects on your health.

Some psychological effects of bullying collected by Carolyn Ashton (1999) include:

- Shattered self-confidence
- Impoverished interpersonal skills
- Impaired communication skills
- Increased sensitivity
- Sense of unworthiness
- Unusually strong feelings of guilt and shame.

She goes on to list the physical symptoms of stress induced by bullying:

- Excessive constant tiredness, listlessness, and fatigue
- Headaches/migraine
- Loss of sex drive/libido
- Excessive or compulsive picking or scratching

- Poor skin quality, irritations, e.g. athletes' foot/psoriasis
- Disturbed sleeping patterns
- Unusual hormonal changes
- Unsettled stomach from butterflies and trembliness to being sick
- Irritable bowel syndrome.

Most victims of bullying in the workplace would claim they could distinguish between bullying behaviours and being robustly managed. The purpose of management includes concepts such as resource control, goal achievement, optimisation or production and can be attained either by individual effort or teamwork. The concepts of bullying are much simpler and revolve around the bullies need to control others. The ultimate purpose of bullying is for gratification of the individual and survival.

## Why does bullying and harassment happen?

According to 'Conflict Management Plus' organisational factors may be cited as contributing significantly to bullying.

## Adversarial, highly competitive organisational culture

- Structural or cultural change
- Long hours culture
- Increase of external/market pressures
- Collusion/avoidance – particularly at senior level
- Lack of support for people experiencing and delivering bullying behaviours
- Physical and emotional resources limited or drained
- Low commitment to equality of opportunity
- Inadequate interpersonal skills training.

## Possible signs of a bullying culture in the workplace

- High staff sickness and turnover
- Weak human resources department – unwilling/unable to tackle bullying in the work force

- No policies and training on harassment, equal opportunities in management
- Obvious nepotism and established favourites
- Dictatorial and controlling management style prevalent.

### The bullying bosses test – is your boss a bully?

According to Sandi Mann (2002) writing in 'Managing your boss' some signs that you may have a bullying boss are included in the following behaviours. Read through this list and tick off.

### How many experience regularly

| | |
|---|---|
| Your boss is prone to exploding angrily | ❏ |
| Your boss picks on you and others unfairly | ❏ |
| Your boss humiliates you in front of others | ❏ |
| Your boss pressures you into doing things you don't want to do or doing things their way | ❏ |
| Your boss has power over you – they can fire you if you don't do what they want | ❏ |
| Your boss constantly ridicules you | ❏ |
| Your boss belittles your achievements | ❏ |

You do not need to experience all of these behaviours to realise you are being bullied. These behaviours constitute bullying if they are continued rather than one off. Other behaviours can also be apparent with a bullying boss but the main purpose of them is to reduce your confidence in your abilities, create anxiety and stress and hit on your self-esteem. They also can leave you feeling isolated and losing confidence in your performance and abilities.

### Who gets bullied?

The UK National Workplace Bullying Advice Line statistics for the period of 1 January 1996 through to 31 January 2002 state that workplace bullying is a global phenomenon. The top four groups as recipients of bullying behaviour are teachers, nurses, social workers and workers in the charity/not for profit/voluntary sector.

Ninety per cent of cases involve a manager bullying a subordinate, 8% are peer to peer bullying and 2% are subordinates bullying their manager. Over 50% of reported bullies are female, probably due to the fact that teaching, nursing and social work have higher than average percentage of female managers. The only apparent difference – (according to the Bullying advice lines respondents) between male and female bullies is that females make much worse bullies than men. 'Bullying is not a gender issue' it claims – bullies may prefer same-sex targets on the basis one knows one's own gender and weak spots. Intelligent bullies also like to remain outside the provisions of the Sex Discrimination Act.

## Why me: are you a victim of bullying?

Maree was a successful assistant to a popular team manager in the health service who was abruptly removed from their post and replaced by a new manager who bullied Maree. She believes she was targeted for her perceived loyalty to her former boss.

'On the first day my replacement manager lined my colleagues and me up and asked us openly to pledge allegiance to her – it was a crazy situation. I couldn't do it. From then on she targeted me and undermined me at every opportunity.'

Maree believed she experienced bullying due to her new manager's insecurity and need to control the team. Over the following months she described being split off from her peers, her responsibilities shrinking, feeling 'left out of the loop' and being told less and less information – which left her feeling that she was no longer part of the team.

According to excerpts from 'Success Unlimited' Maree may have become ideal 'bully fodder' because of trigger events.

- Re-organisation
- She had a new manager appointed
- Obvious displays of affection and respect or trust from co-workers
- Refusing to obey an order – in this case a public pledge of allegiance.

Personal qualities that Maree displayed and bullies find 'irresistible' include:

- Popularity
- Idealism
- Competence

- Being slow to anger
- Honesty and integrity
- Being helpful
- Trustworthy and trusting
- Sensitivity
- Giving and selfless
- Difficulty saying 'No'.

Jane realised she had been bullied only after she had left her position as a personal assistant. 'It was my second position, and I was young and naïve and eager to please. My boss was an older male and made personal and derogatory remarks about my physical appearance. I was to hurt and embarrassed to say anything. He commented on my nose and mouth and said I looked like a boxer, as my nose has been broken as a child I was very sensitive to this and other personal comments. I don't know why I put up with it.'

Jane displayed further personal qualities that bullies find 'irresistible' such as:

- Tolerance
- An inability to value oneself whilst attributing greater importance and validity to other people's opinions of oneself
- A strong forgiving streak and desire to think well of others
- Low assertiveness
- Internalising anger rather than expressing it.

Jane found it hard to believe she was being bullied and had concluded the behaviour was light-hearted if unwanted office banter; she claimed she felt awkward about challenging it at the time and felt she would be labelled as insensitive, naïve or not able to take a joke. Jane's solution was to leave this position and only years later is she able to label her experience as 'bullying'.

Sandy would have described herself as both competent and confident. Moving to a new senior position within the health service, she joined a newly merged organisation. She was popular with her peers and looking forwarded to the challenge of her new role. Her bullying experience started from her first performance appraisal – where the feedback was so negative as to be both undermining and belittling to her former confidence and personality. She described feeling 'gagged' when contributing in meetings and later described 'it was as if what I contributed was of no value'. She was soon asked to attend fortnightly performance monitoring meetings – where she felt routinely criticised and picked on her performance, in the privacy of the 'bullies' office.

Sandy described becoming aware that her external perception as a manager was being undermined as she was excluded from information and was finding herself not being invited to relevant meetings. Members of her team were given time privately and exclusively by the bully where her performance was discussed. Not unexpectedly her profile internally and externally as a competent manager began to diminish.

Sandy began to doubt her own competency and abilities. Her staff appeared to know more than she did about strategic decisions. Questions about her ability to lead her team began being circulated and 'subordinate to manager' bullying began to surface.

Sandy felt she was targeted because of her initial confidence in her own abilities. She was seen as a highflier and therefore was perceived as a threat. She also described herself as popular and likeable with a number of friends in her peer groups at work. Sandy also believed her questioning style was seen as insubordinate and disloyal.

Sandy had unwittingly become bully fodder by some of her behaviours:

- Refusing to join a clique/showing independence of thought
- Being popular with colleagues/customers/clients/patients
- Challenging the status quo, especially unwittingly.

Bullying can occur at any time in one's career as shown by the experiences of Maree – middle manager in an established team, Jane – a junior member in an established team and Sandy – a senior member in a new organisation. Each one of them was subjected to bullying behaviours of varying degrees by events that triggered bullying and the bullies need to 'bully and seek control'. Bullies are predatory and opportunistic and you can happen to be in the wrong place at the wrong time. However, some behaviour's can trigger and worsen bullying and qualities that the victim possesses that contributed to this may be the ones that conversely make the victims initially popular.

These include:

- Slowness to anger
- Giving and selfless nature
- Difficulty saying 'No'
- Diligent, industrious
- Tolerance
- Strong sense of humour
- Quick to apologise
- A strong desire to be reasonable
- High coping skills.

## Why do women put up with it?

Carolyn Ashton (1999) cited 'there are a number of reasons why bullying behaviour is often tolerated in the workplace ...'.

*Lack of recognition* – Women may be anxious to name what is happening to them for fear of being ridiculed or labelled oversensitive – particularly if the bully is older, well established and respected. CJ described an experience where a subordinate became bullying and intimidating in front of her eyes. 'He lowered his voice and made derogatory comments about my management style and made me feel physically threatened. I had been trying to give him feedback on his performance in which others had found him intimidating and he turned it on me. This pleasant, gentle, professional middle manager became an aggressive rude and a threatening ogre in my office. Speaking to peers afterwards they found it hard to believe my experience, as he was normally so differential and much older than me. He'd taken early retirement and commenced a much junior position in all areas of customer relations, afterwards I understood his move down the ladder.' Under pressure his bullying nature became apparent.

For some bullies they are able to hide their behaviours so well the target reporting them is initially disbelieved. However, bullies rarely strike once, and after some digging a history of similar behaviours is usually unearthed.

*Professionalism* – People and especially those good at their jobs/take pride in their work and try hard to avoid criticism and attack. They may feel walking away is letting the bully win. This professionalism can cause women to remain in the work environment to keep trying to prove their worth.

*Financial incentives* – As the sole or equal breadwinners, women often need to work to support their family's expenditure. Therefore, confronting the bully especially if they have hiring/firing powers is too high a risk for the family.

*Loyalty and commitment* – To one's place of employment, if the job was enjoyable before the bullying, hope is often placed in the fact the bully may leave, change or find another target.

*Desire to care for those in ones charge* – (e.g. patients, inmates, children) or junior staff. Women often feel the need to protect and care for others and this may be tapped into by the bully and used against them.

*The support of colleagues* – Having a 'bully' in the office can be the focus for negative energy. Teamwork can develop to support the bullied or to share experiences and commiserate. Being the current target can generate more support and this in turn can build peer support (in some, not all cases) making it hard to leave the area/workplace.

## Bullying vs Harassment

At present if you are being bullied and you are white, British, able bodied and the same gender as the bully you are not covered under discrimination law. There is very little protection in legal terms afforded to those who experience bullying in the workplace.

The Protection from the Harassment Act (1996) has influenced employer's awareness and accords emphasis for the first time on the target's perception of harassment rather than the perpetrators alleged intent. Harassment and bullying differ in several ways, though there is much overlap.

Harassment often has a physical component and may include intrusive contact in a physical sense but also intrusion into personal space and possessions. There is focus on the individual due to differences such as gender; sexuality and offensive vocabulary may be used to belittle the victim publicly.

Harassment takes place in and out of work and the harasser may occur for peer approval, i.e. to prove a macho image. Bullying in the workplace is often more subtle and is usually exclusively psychological, based on trivial criticisms and allegations of under performance. It is the far more secretive act carried out behind closed doors without witnesses, the victim may not even realise they are being bullied until much later. The typical workplace bully will lack social and interpersonal skills. They may realise their reputation as a 'difficult to work for' boss and believe this is due to them being a perfectionist and demanding high standard's which the target simply cannot meet.

### What can you do if you find you are being bullied?

In asking a group of women this question the most consistent response was 'tell someone about it!' Women in general find sharing experiences whether good or bad a helpful exercise and part of that is to validate the feelings you are having.

### Speak up!

This depends on what you intend to do about the situation. Sharing your experience with a work colleague can be a way of ensuring others note what is happening to you but only if the colleague is unlikely to side with the bully or repeat the behaviour. If the bully is the boss speaking to your human resources department in confidence, your trade union representative or if your employer has a 'whistle blowing' policy – seeking out the designated lead for your areas are all possibilities. It's also a good idea to have a witness or representative with you so you can clarify what you said and any information/advice given to you. Keep notes of the dates and times you spoke to management about your experience.

### Best tip

Keep detailed written notes of all conversations with the bully and who and when you approached people or professional organisations for help. These may be vital pieces of evidence if you decide to take up a grievance with your employer at some stage.

### Speak to the bullies line manager

This is a high-risk strategy. It can and has stopped bullies in their tracks but if the bully is senior and established and has a close relationship with their line manager it is not an advisable strategy. If the bully has a history of bullying and the organisation wants to 'shed' them you may find yourself central to the case and your views will count. If the bully is not aware of the impact of their behaviour on you – having a manager speak to them about your perceptions has in some cases been effective.

### Talk to peers outside of the work situation

They may not be able to help directly but you can off load to them and friends can help balance the situation. It's easy to become sensitive and overly focused on your experiences. You need to create a work life balance and getting perspectives from others outside of the workplace, especially if you work in a specialist field, can be an advantage at times.

### Reduce contact time with the bully

If possible try and remove yourself from 'target practice'. Avoid the bully but not your work responsibilities. Keep communication clear and if possible communicate in public or by email and keep all your records. A clever bully will be aware of the ability to keep and forward emails so their behaviours may be curtailed. Ensure you clarify information they give you and ask for written feedback. You may not get it – but they may be more wary if they know you keep records of requests. Keep focused on the job. Stay very polite.

### Take care of yourself

Being the target of a bully can seriously affect you health. This is the time to review your diet and alcohol intake. Ensure your diet is high in vegetables and fruit, that you take lunch breaks and leave work at a reasonable hour. You may find your sleep patterns are affected and this in tern effects your productivity and alertness at work. Make sure you switch off from work stress by turning mobile phones and pagers off where possible. Also try not to take work home with you.

### Best tip

Use the journey home to unwind so once at home the bully doesn't 'come too'. Ensure you have a routine that enables you to leave work problems at work – leave your briefcase at the door, mobile switched off and change out of work clothes.

### Seek counselling

If the bullying behaviour impacts on your self-esteem and confidence or you develop physical symptoms such as – insomnia, panic attacks, phobias, avoidance of situations, ruminations or depression, consider seeking professional help. Your occupational health department can refer you and there may be confidential schemes attached to your company. Alternatively your union may provide a counseling or advisory service. Your employer has a duty to ensure your health and welfare under the Health and Safety at Work Act (1974) More recently a discussion document *Managing Stress at Work* (1999) indicates that if advice is not followed by employers on a voluntary basis then the HS Executive may introduce a statutory 'Approved Code of Practice' which would make employers liable to a criminal prosecution.

### Best tip
Don't let life become unbearable through bullying and cumulative stress before asking for help. You are worth more; your health is worth more – treat yourself well and expect everyone else to do so to.

### Assertiveness training
Consider if your manner is allowing the bully to intimidate you. Are you allowing the bully access to you because you are compliant, tolerant and overly helpful? Consider taking assertiveness training and ask trusted friends for feedback on your demeanour and whether you are falling into the target zone because of being too nice.

### Sometimes you have to walk away
At the end of the day remember it's 'only a job'. As Maree decided after feeling undermined by her new boss and made to feel devalued – leaving her position was a positive option – 'so I wasn't left mentally and physically exhausted'. Maree joined another organisation that appreciated her skills and helped restore her confidence.

Knowing when to walk away is an important choice – don't compromise or sacrifice so much because of bullying behaviours that you can't enjoy your job or position. Choosing to leave can be an act of assertion and enable you to move to a more positive environment. Working should be a stimulating and financially rewarding part of your life – if being targeted has reduced this – remember you don't have to stay and suffer.

### Best tip
Sometimes you may choose to walk away. You can only fight so much. Know what your limits are and start accumulating 'Get out of hell money' enough so you can leave if you have to – when you need to. Having some financial padding can enable you to leave an unworkable situation.

### Stress management
Working as a woman outside of the home – though often rewarding, demanding and challenging can when combined with our other roles of partner, carer, daughter, lover friend, and parent – make us feel overwhelmed at times. Whatever role you are in, you will at times, feel that you are doing a disservice to another role or barely covering all the bases.

Stress has been described as 'The gap between what you want and what you actually have!' Most of us can identify the physical symptoms of stress – we have experienced panicky feelings through to insomnia and anxiety attacks. Most of us are able to identify that stress in our lives is a combination of events in our work or private lives that makes us feel overloaded.

Below is a compilation of stress-busting ideas to help when the going gets tough.

## 25 best stress-busters tips

### Take a holiday

Your perspective can become terribly narrowed when in a crisis. You envision you are in a long dark tunnel and you ruminate and relive the events that are bothering you. A holiday can radically blow away the clouds and allow your perspective to come back. Never underestimate the affect of tiredness on your moods.

### Try something different

Be an experience mercenary. Visit a local art gallery, go to the theatre, and take a day off mid-week. Change your hairstyle/lose weight – change can help reduce the feeling of being in a rut – and get you out of your routine.

### Say 'No'

Don't keep doing what you've always done – when you feel overwhelmed take control in other areas of your life:

- Send supermarket cakes to the Scouts end-of-year event
- If you are having friends/family over dinner, tell them to each bring a course, don't be the martyr in the kitchen
- Don't volunteer if you don't want to – decline elegantly
- Hire a cleaner – keep your weekends free and pay someone to do your ironing.

### Start a journal

Writing down your progress and keeping a record of feelings is one of the best ways to keep centred in a crisis. You can note your feelings and coping strategies and realise how far you have come.

You can also list patterns and record when your experiencing problems how you feel and what helps. Journaling is a powerful way to record your coping strategies and experiences

## *Talk*

Especially good for the 'counsellors' in us – out there. If you are the fixer, sorter, problem-solver type who is often leaned on, it can be liberating to offload and swap roles. Find a trusted friend and spill the beans. Allow yourself to receive support.

## *Volunteer*

Like to try something different? Volunteer for something you want to do, not out of guilt or social pressure. Mentoring is a popular area where your experiences can help adolescents in a range of situations. Share your knowledge and increase your confidence and competence quota at the same time.

## *Don't always be nice*

As Kate White writing in '*Why good girls don't get ahead but gutsy girls do!*' She advocates that women should not always follow the rules. White advocates just because its never been done before doesn't mean you can't do it, and just because someone says you shouldn't doesn't mean you can't.

Consider cutting corners, saying no, saying yes, and not waiting for the perfect time – jump in – ready or not!

## *Read*

Reading can be a way of immersing yourself in a different space for a while. It can be an avoidance but also a way of recharging your batteries. Reading can be a way of having experiences and developing your knowledge whilst not leaving your home or role – it can also give you private time and be used as a people excluder when commuting! Don't underestimate the power of a good book to lift your mood and take you out of yourself. Consider joining a library or starting a book circle where you review books with a group of friends.

## *Music*

Loud music whether opera, rock, R&B or even Christmas carols can blast the cobwebs out and be therapeutic. Trying to feel down when listening to Aretha Franklin belting out 'Respect' is difficult. Use music on that home journey to help bring closure to the day.

## Baking or cooking

For some women this fulfils the need to nurture and is relaxing. Whether you're a 'goddess' or simply god-awful in the kitchen – cooking can be pleasurable if it's done at your leisure, uninterrupted and for your enjoyment. Some women feel it can bring a sense of achievement also.

## Spend time with children

Either yours or borrow some! Their irreverence, need for attention, sense of silliness are all absorbing. Children can help blow away the storm clouds – especially if involved in a physical activity – a long walk, take them swimming or visit a zoo. Do something that needs your full attention and arrange your day so you can give it. Bliss!

## Exercise

Not one of my favourites – but if you're a gymphopbic like myself – long walks in bracing weather are a great way to life the blues or ruminations. Exercise increases endorphins, a natural stimulant, which help to raise your mood by increasing positive hormones.

## Balance

Are you doing too much? If you're reading this you probably are! Slow down - learn to drop a few of the balls you're juggling. Your health and state of mind being in balance are more important that 'sweating the small stuff' as Anthony Robbin's, writes 'It's all small stuff.' Take a holiday minus your work phone – and leave work on time consistently.

## Treat yourself

The usual suggestions of candles/baths/massage – have been well documented and used in the last 10 years. Find what you enjoy doing and do it. Favourites collected include shopping on your own, buying books, a good cappuccino and a trashy magazine or a quickie manicure, lengthy facial and trying out lots of new cosmetics!

## Feng Shui

A lot has been written about the principles of Feng shui. In Lillian Too's book *Feng Shui at Work* (1999) she advocates designing your workspace to promote health and well being, reduce negative energies and enliven your environment.

Using plants with rounded leaves, sitting your desk in the most appropriate corner, using light to attract energy, using mirrors correctly all help to make a more harmonious and stress free environment in which to work. Consider making your work environment as pleasant as your home to reduce stress in this area.

### *Try therapy*

When your mood is not coming up, or if you feel your self-esteem/confidence is in your boots or you have contemplated self-harming or have suicidal thoughts – consider getting professional help. Life is not to be endured but enjoyed.

### *Set goals*

Set 'small smart' goals to get you through when the going is tough. Each tick can be therapeutic which is why the smart 'specific, measurable, attainable, realistic and time-orientated' goals are so important. Even in the worst situation try and move forward, whether on the work front or making a date to see friends. Goals can also be rewards for completing difficult tasks.

### *Reward*

Depending on your budget – treat yourself. From a manicure to a ticket to a concert. Or buy time – have a friend take the kids and you return the favour, use this time to shop, plan and take a weekend break or simply read but make it a positive experience.

### *Study*

Is there something you want to know more about? A subject you want to look into – a qualification, you must have! Studying is a focus that enables some women to learn new skills and change direction. Or develop a hobby or interest further. Local universities and further education colleges offer night classes, which are often short and provide a taster in a range of subject areas.

### *Renovate*

Think about the rooms you live in – do they serve a purpose? Does the colour scheme soothe or motivate? Is an ambience created? Find your style and stick to it. Develop a sample of styles by ripping out colours/details from home style/lifestyle magazines and devise your stratagems for creating an environment you want to come home too. Think about colour/texture/smell – in your new environment.

### Donate

You know the rule – if it has not been out of your wardrobe for a year – out it goes – permanently! Do not keep clothes that you need to lose 5Ibs to fit into. They remind you of a slimmer you! Instead most high streets have a plethora of charity shops to donate too. Unclutter and be altruistic at the same time.

### Garden

If you do not have a garden – try a window box. Growing something from seeds or cuttings is very rewarding and can be therapeutic. It needs a little time, some attention and can result in a creation, whether it is an entire flowerbed or a group of well-fed African Violets.

### Change

Small is good when already under stress – so moving house is not advisable, but you could change your hair colour, the coffee you drink, the café you have lunch at, your route to work. Variety can lift you out of a rut and help stop ruminating and dreaming of what you haven't got.

### Sleep

Lack of sleep or sustained periods of broken sleep is one of the best ways to lose perspective. When you are tired it is easy to feel run down, make mistakes through lost concentration and generally feeling like the world is against you. A good nights sleep is essential to remain balanced. Use lavender oils on your pillow or a few drops distilled into carrier oil and rubbed onto temples before bed.

### Count your blessings

You are a woman, with great potential, courage and self-worth – going through a difficult period – but life is still great!

## References

Ashton, C. (1999) *Bullying and Harassment in the Workplace*. Notes from seminar held on 15 June, London.

*Conflict Management Plus*, Issue 9, handout.

Field, T. (1999) *Bully in Sight* (UK, Success Unlimited).

Health and Safety Commission (1999) *Managing Stress at Work*. Discussion document.

Mann, S. (2002) *Managing your Boss in a Week* (UK, Hodder and Stoughton).

Robbins, A. (1989) *Unlimited Power* (UK, Simon and Schuster).

Toos, L. (1999) *Little Book of Feng Shui at Work* (UK, Element Books Ltd).

White, K. (1998) *Why Good Girls don't get ahead... but Gutsy Girls do* (UK, Century).


## Useful Websites

www.successunlimited.co.uk/bully/

www.suzylamplugh.org/home/aboutus

www.stress.org.uk

www.isma.org.uk

Bullying online (the wesbite of UK National Workplace Bullying Advice Line)


## Useful Publications

Andrea, A. (1992) *Bullying at Work* (UK, Virago).

Covey, R.S. (1994) *First Things First* (UK, Simon and Shuster).

Goleman, D. (1996) *Emotional Intelligence* (UK, Bloomsbury).

Harrold, F. (2000) *Be your own Life Coach* (UK, Hodder & Stoughton).

Kinchin, D. (2001) *Post Traumatic Stress Disorder* (UK, Success Unlimited).

White, K. (1998) *The 9 Secrets of Women who get what they want...* (UK, Century Random House).

# Chapter 9
## Work-Life Balance, Flexi-time and Working from Home

**Anna M. Maslin**

We all sometimes feel life is getting out of control. None of us have unlimited time and yet many of us feel as if we have unlimited responsibilities. It is often very difficult for men and women to balance time and responsibilities. There is also the 'long hours culture' that sometimes pervades the corridors of power whether real or imagined. Many women feel they must apologise for their responsibilities and their lives in the work place. This doesn't just apply to women with children but also to women who have other responsibilities, whether it is wider family, civil society or just to themselves. Health and well-being are important and there are now opportunities and options available to employers and employees, which at one time would have been thought of as unthinkable.

The government in the UK is committed to helping us all recognise that work-life balance is a real issue and one where staff and employers need to work together to improve the situation. The aim is to raise employer's awareness to the business benefits of helping employees create a better balance between work and the rest of their lives. A good working relationship with an employer should result in increased productivity, a higher degree of commitment and a reduced incidence of sickness absence due to stress or stress related illness. We are all different. We all work in quite different ways and we all expect different things from our work environment.

In order to think through what might be possible it is worth noting the range of options the UK government is putting forward as possibilities. Options, which could be available to employees, are;

**Flexi-time**

Flexi-time which gives people the choice about exactly what their actual working hours are. Often built into this are either core hours or core days when people agree to meet together on corporate business.

Flexi-time has been one of the innovations, which have been around longer than some of the others. It acknowledges that people work better at different times of the day and allows this flexibility to maximise productivity. The flexibility also ensures that if an employee needs to be at home or elsewhere because of another commitment this can be accommodated without either their work or their personal life suffering.

Core hours or days are usually agreed in advance with the employer enabling everyone to feel that ring-fenced time is available for meetings or corporate work.

**Staggered hours**

Staggered hours are where employees are able to start and finish at different times.

Staggered hours are really just a variation of flexi-time and have similar benefits provided there is true employer/employee negotiation. Staggered hours however could have a negative effect if the system is not negotiated and employees are forced to be available early mornings or late evenings when other responsibilities could be compromised.

**Time off in lieu**

Time off in lieu is where employees and employers agree time can be taken off at a mutually convenient time for extra hours worked.

This is very good in principle but on occasion it can be found that the employee is never allowed the time off. There never seems to be a convenient time for the employer or the time offered is not commensurate with the time given.

**Part-time work**

This is work, which is less in hours than full-time employment. Some people define it as less than 30 hours a week.

Part-time work has been the main flexible option women have traditionally opted for in combining paid work with home responsibilities. This can be very effective and satisfying but often women feel their salary level has been affected by this choice.

## Job sharing

Job sharing where two people share one job and divide the pay holidays and other benefits. Each person is employed part-time but together they cover a full-time post.

This can work very well where you have two people and their management committed to ensuring its success. Key points to consider are the compatibility of the job sharers, their long term aims and objectives, how they will manage their staff and any issues where staff appear to be playing off one person against the other. On the up side some of the positions offering job-share opportunities can be at very senior levels with the appropriate salary attached.

## Home working

This allows an individual to work all or part of their time from a homework space.

Home working allows an individual to use their home as an office to carry out their work responsibilities. For home working to be successful there needs to be a number of elements in place. These include:

### An employer who is supportive and trusts you

If your employer is unhappy with the arrangement they are unlikely to be supportive. If they are not supportive you may feel that you are being constantly questioned and held to account. If on the other hand your employer is happy with the arrangement and is supportive you will find you are able to work productively with few problems

### An employee who is trustworthy and gets their work done

Home working is not suited to everyone and an employer would be foolish to allow someone who is not achieving their business objectives at work because they are not as focused as they might be to be at home where distractions could be magnified. A person who works well in the office is equally capable of working well at home.

### An employee who does not need to have people around constantly to feel valued

This is an important issue. For some people the need for social interaction and the ability to run ideas by a living breathing colleague is essential. For those individuals working alone can be a nightmare. They miss the camaraderie of day-to-day interaction with colleagues at work. Others on the other hand are quite content to progress their work with the addition of planned face-to-face meetings supplemented by email and telephone.

### A suitable work environment

This is important. To work effectively you will need the appropriate tools including an appropriate space. You can work anywhere in the world provided you have access to a telephone, a fax and a PC. Should one fail you can always use the other. Home workers need to know their employers policy on how they requisition items and how they are reimbursed for allowable expenses, etc. They also need to be aware of any tax implications as a result of their home working.

### Regular hours or a way of being contacted at all work times. If you are working at home you need to be available

Home workers need to be available to their employers and clients during working hours. Nothing will compromise your being allowed to continue to work at home if people cannot get hold of you. On the other side though often people usually do know how to get hold of you and you can find you are being contacted day and night particularly if you have international clients or colleagues. Strategies and appropriate handling of this situation from the beginning will help ensure everyone is content. A reliable messaging service for whenever you are unavailable is important. Whatever suits use. If you don't have a secretary a remote access answering machine or other messaging service that you check regularly.

### Good childcare

Working from home may mean you can drop the children off at school or collect them but you will not be able to look after them during work hours. The children need quality time and your time needs to be spent on your work. Sometimes employers and employees think working from home means you can look after the children too. You can't. Children require attention and your attention needs to be on your work. You may agree with your employer that you work flexi-time during the day so you can spend some time with a small child during the day and then that time is made up, often in the early evening.

### Regular updates are important. Let people know what you are doing

Employers and other colleagues sometimes find it easy to say 'oh so and so does nothing at home' because they fail to see the product of your work. Regular updates and regular forward plans, which are widely circulated, are a very useful way of managing the situation and keeping everyone up-to-date.

### Flexibility.
### Both the employee and employer need to be willing to compromise

Although there are some people who work exclusively from home many employees now interchange main office and home office working on occasions. In my work I may be away from home overseas for a week or so at a time because of this I appreciate being able to work from home days either side of a trip so that my family get to see me too. Employees who work at home for the majority of their time should show some flexibility in order to ensure business objectives are met.

I have now worked from home at times for the last four years after the birth of my third child. My main office is in London, my home office is in Bournemouth, one hundred miles away from each other, and I travel a great deal for work both nationally and internationally. Home working has meant for me that I don't have to get up every day at 5:00 a.m. and come home at 8:00 p.m. or later. It means I can see my children in the morning and have dinner with them in the evening. It means that although I still have to employ childcare I can be physically close if I'm needed.

Home working isn't for everyone but I think it is becoming more widely recognised as a valid and effective way of improving working lives for many people particularly now housing is so expensive in many major cities. It can also provide a very useful way of maximising official office space. For me home working has been an excellent way of achieving a healthier work-life balance.

For further information visit:
www.dti.gov.uk/work-lifebalance

Flexible Working Arrangements
Equal Opportunities Commission
Information advice including publications
Tel: 0161 833 9244
www.eoc.org.uk

Flametree
Information and advice
Tel: 020 7376 0618
www.flameree.co.uk

Flexecutive
Experts in the field of flexible working
Tel: 020 7636 6744
www.flexecutive.co.uk

New Ways to Work
Information advice and publications
Helpline: 020 7503 3578
www.new-ways.co.uk

Parents at Work
Information, advice and publications
Tel: 20 7628 2128/3578
www.parents@work.org

# Chapter 10
## A Personal View...

### Heather Angel

#### Working for yourself

As the sun dips towards the horizon, a huge white ice arch becomes suffused with a pink glow. In front of this amazing backdrop hundreds of emperor penguins huddle together as the temperature plummets to −30°C. It had taken me almost 2 weeks to reach this part of Antarctica in an ice breaker and several hours trudging over the ice to reach this spot, but I knew this moment would live with me forever. As I savoured the pristine wilderness, I reflected that had I chosen another path as a career I would never have experienced this magical moment.

By the time I married Martin (a fellow zoologist) at the age of twenty-three, I presumed I would carve out a career as a marine biologist for life. After all, I had a zoology degree and had been doing marine biological research for three years. I never dreamt I would abandon my love for the marine world and develop an even greater passion for photography. Yet, it was only a few years later that I took the plunge to work as a freelance wildlife photographer.

#### Why work for yourself?

The prime reason why most women work is quite simply to earn money to survive, or to help support a growing family. Work can be so much more pleasurable if you are lucky enough to find a job that you relish. But not everyone can be so lucky. Working for yourself is an option that deserves consideration for doing what you enjoy when you want to do it.

Without a job specification in black and white, how do you decide where to start? Life's path is a plethora of crossroads; arguably never more so than when debating what to do when contemplating working for yourself. The most obvious springboard may be a life-long interest or hobby; but it could equally well arise from reading an article or even overhearing a chance comment on the radio or on television.

A good starting point is to jot down what you enjoy doing (although in reality it may prove not possible or practical to develop this into a way of earning money). One lady I know began catering for friends' dinner parties and within a few years had developed a most productive business branching out into commercial as well as private catering with her own distinctive van. If you enjoy writing, overheads are minimal when starting up as a freelance writer; although it will help if you are computer literate.

But working for yourself is by no means a bed of roses. I have listed the pro's and con's (see below) from my own experience of working as a self-employed photographer for 30 years.

### Pro's

- You will be your own boss
- Can choose your own work schedule
- Can work around the family
- Can work at what interests you
- Can dress as you please – except when meeting clients
- Can stop working when you choose.

### Con's

- You have to generate the workload and work out priorities
- No guaranteed monthly salary
- You will have to learn how to keep necessary records (both income and expenditure) so that profit and loss accounts can be assessed at the end of your tax year
- Learn how to say no to social invites which clash with your business demands

- You will need to set yourself goals
- You will have to learn – and learn fast – how to sell yourself and promote your business
- You will need to look ahead to the future
- If you become ill, you will not have an income unless you take out an insurance policy.

## Feasibility study

Having a dream is one thing, but how do you make this become a reality? Before you take the plunge, here are a few queries you should ponder.

- What type of business appeals to you?
- Can you identify who would want to buy your product or use your services?
- Have you researched a gap in the market that you could fill?
- Have you discussed your aspirations with your partner, family or friends?
- Will you need a bank loan or other funding to get the business started?
- How will you promote your business?
- Have you set yourself 6-month and first year achievable turnover targets?
- Have you costed your expenses for the first year?

If you covered the last two points, then it will not be too difficult to produce a written business plan, which is essential for obtaining a bank loan.

## Time-savers

Whatever path you choose to take and however you achieve the launch of a business, you then have to think constantly of ways and means of achieving your goals. This is always tougher when you are a sole trader; whereas if you decide to go into business as a partnership, you do at least have someone else to bounce off ideas and to discuss the way ahead. Balancing a budget is important, but so is being organised and thinking ahead of ways and means of saving time.

Nothing annoys me more than wasting time standing in queues – whether it be in a supermarket, a bank or at a railway station. So here are a few ways in which I avoid queues.

- Shop late (or very early) in a 24-hour supermarket to avoid check-out queues.
- Avoid going to a bank at lunch-time, when the staff are reduced and full-time workers converge on banks.
- Book rail tickets over the 'phone or on the internet. They will either be posted or can be collected from the station.

Whenever I go on a train or plane journey, I make sure that I utilise the downtime to the full by having a thick pad and plenty of pens (less weight than a laptop and quicker for me to input) packed in my briefcase the night before. This is how I write most of my articles and books and also jot down promotion ideas. I am fortunate in having a PA who deciphers my scribbles and inputs them into a computer.

## Organise your day

As women, we are fortunate in having the ability to multi-task, which is a huge asset whether working for a company or for yourself. Whether you live on your own or have a family, it is essential to organise your time efficiently, to slot in the essential domestic tasks – such as shopping, cooking and transporting children - into your working day.

I chose to write this 'personal view' on Good Friday, a day when I knew both the 'phone and the fax would stop ringing and I could ignore my emails (I get between 15–20 a day).

Much to my husband's merriment, I have always been an avid list maker. Firstly, this helps not only to make sure I don't miss one of the many deadlines set me daily, but also it enables me to prioritise the jobs. Secondly, it gives me great satisfaction to cross off each job as it is completed.

My list today reads:

- Write copy for *Tips for Women at Work*
- Edit and caption elephant pictures from Botswana
- Compile two digital lightboxes for a US client
- Call USA re hummingbird workshop
- Scan new pictures to upload on website.

At first glance this list may appear rather daunting, but the last three tasks are not at all time-consuming. Digital lightboxes are compiled by going to my website, selecting relevant images for each client, who is sent an automated email for them to pull the images up on their screen from my server. Scanning slides is now much less time-consuming because I can scan them in batches of five at a time. After putting them in the holder I press two buttons and then revert to another task, returning after they have all been scanned to correct the colour and add the correct file name.

## Promoting yourself

Some people shy away from promoting themselves; but if you are going to make a success of working for yourself it is essential that you let people know you exist and what you have to offer. Chapter 2 is devoted to how to write your CV when applying for a job. Once successful, the CV is invariably moth-balled until you decide to apply for another job, when it is hastily updated.

From experience as a self-employed person, I know how just how essential it is to keep my CV constantly updated, because I never know when it will be needed. So as soon as I return from an overseas trip, have a new book published, do a TV interview or an exhibition is staged at a new venue, my CV is updated. During the first four months of 2003 I cannot recall how many times it has been dispatched around the world. It all started in Beijing in February when an exhibition of my work opened. I was besieged by the press, and many glossy magazines wanted to produce features on my work. A call to my office (I have a mobile I can use from China) ensured my CV was emailed to each publication. Since then, I have been asked to lecture and run a week's workshop in Singapore and the organiser needed my CV to help him promote the event.

Another useful way to promote yourself is to take note whenever a client expresses pleasure and satisfaction with your work, ask them for a quote to use on a leaflet or on the internet (when you get your own website).

You only have to walk past the magazine section in a newsagents to appreciate just how many titles are now published. It would be difficult to think of a topic that does not have its own specialist magazine. While most magazines have regular writers, there is always scope for getting free publicity in the news pages. We regularly send off press releases to the photographic press. These used to be in print form, but now we send them as an email. Essentially you need a punchy eye-catching title, a few paragraphs of copy and, preferably, a relevant photo. The following release appeared (with a photo of the puffin) in every magazine we emailed with all my contact details (which have been omitted for publication here).

---

**PRESS RELEASE**

## Winning Puffin

Heather Angel has won the Animal Antics category in the prestigious International Photography Awards organised by the US magazine *Nature's Best*. Her winning shot depicts a puffin in flight with legs and tail askew in an Icelandic gale.

Angel relates the story:

"In July 2001 I went to Iceland specifically to take puffins in flight. Strong winds are normally bad for photography. One day when a gale was blowing I almost turned back, but on climbing up to the cliff top I noted virtually all the puffins were hunkered down against the persistent wind. Not a promising start to a photo session! Suddenly an extra strong gust of wind blew a puffin off the cliff and it hung hawk-like just above the ground with its legs and tail askew. I was able to take several frames before the bird descended out of sight."

---

## Safety aspects

In recent years, several women have approached me regarding the safety aspect of my job, which takes me to remote parts of Britain and around the world. I usually reply with the following advice:

- When venturing to a remote place on your own, make sure someone knows where you plan to visit and at what time you expect to return.

- Carry a mobile phone.

- If possible, arrange to meet a local contact who knows the area.

- When travelling abroad remove all jewellery and don't flash expensive cameras in towns and cities.

- Don't carry a conventional handbag abroad; it is too tempting. I distribute my money, travellers cheques and credit cards in different places, which I am not going to divulge here!

## Conclusion

Before you start your own business, talk to as many people as possible, so you will be aware of some of the pitfalls at least. Once you have made the decision to work for yourself, embark with enthusiasm, it is very likely that you will be rewarded with your efforts and be forever grateful that you took the plunge. I am a firm believer that life is what you make it.

**Reference**

Burch, G. (2003) *Go It Alone: The Streetwise Secrets of Self Employment* (London, John Wiley & Sons).

If you have access to the internet and use a search engine such as www.google.co.uk to search for self employment UK several useful websites appear. Notably a most helpful one from the Inland Revenue www.ukonline.gov.uk/startingupinbusiness which gives advice on record keeping, with a help-line number for newly self-employed; also a free appointment can be arranged with the Inland Revenue's Business Support Team.

## Dame Lorna Muirhead

### Introduction

Choice is the word of the moment and many modern women are fortunate that they can exercise it in many ways.

Now reaching the end of my professional life, I belong to the first generation of post-war women who, having the benefit of a good education, went on to pursue a career, married, had a family, and then had to make decisions about how career and family could co-exist.

In my early working days, midwifery, which is my profession, was largely the prerogative of single women who like many others in the NHS, gave unstintingly of themselves to their work. It was very rare to find a married midwife; in fact I was the first one to be employed by my hospital in 1965. Now, over 50% of midwives are married and many have children.

My children were born before the days of statutory maternity leave, therefore, if women had babies they left paid employment, raised their children, usually until school age and then had to decide if and how they were going to return to the workplace.

The need to earn money was not a prime consideration. Lifestyle was more modest and mortgages obtained taking the salary of the husband into account. This meant that the woman's income was not needed to support the basic essentials of living and although money was not in abundance, it was perfectly possible to exist on one salary, unlike today's lifestyle which, though more opulent, often requires a joint income to support it.

It could be said that I had far more choice of whether to return to paid work than many women do today. When I see the pressure on some of my younger colleagues trying to maintain a home and family, whilst having to pursue a full-time job, I sometimes wonder if today's women have been liberated.

When my children were of school age I thought long and hard about what I now wanted from my life which seemed to me to be like a jigsaw, with many pieces making up the whole picture. I loved family life and I valued my profession, so in common with many other women I decided I would try to have both. I became a part-time midwife. This left me enough time in between my days on duty to fulfil my role as housekeeper, wife and mother.

### Advantages of a part-time career

I had a job I loved and was mentally stimulated. I relished the companionship of my colleagues and was making use of my training. Most of all I had an identity. I also had time to have a large input into my children's lives and I was able to manage my domestic commitments. For the first few years I was happy and fulfilled; lucky I thought, to have the best of both worlds.

### Disadvantages of a part-time career

The prevailing attitude of many employers and indeed of some colleagues, was that part-time workers were simply at work to earn 'pin-money'. We were not really ambitious or indeed as dedicated as those who worked full-time, and unlike our full-time colleagues, had no need of professional development, nor promotion. Therefore, we were simply used to provide a service. To be fair, some part-time workers fitted this stereotype, but I was not one of them.

Whilst at work I gave 101% of myself to the job. I kept professionally up-to-date and over many years helped pioneer innovative practices and techniques in my ward. I wrote chapters in midwifery textbooks and was a frequent lecturer at statutory study days and refresher courses for midwives. I was politically aware and professionally informed and engaged in local politics through my local branch of the Royal College of Midwives, where in turn I became it's secretary, chairman, press officer and steward. As an articulate women who hates controversy, but loathes injustice even more, I was able to support colleagues through disciplinary and grievance procedures, becoming an advocate for those midwives less able to defend or speak for themselves. No, I was certainly not at work just for the pin money.

### Problems for me

Coping with the lack of career progression for part-time workers was one of the most difficult tasks I had to face. It wasn't that I wanted promotion for itself, but I felt I had more to give than I was able to do in the position I held. It is true that my clinical skills were valued and that I had much satisfaction from looking after pregnant women, but it is almost impossible to influence anything from the shop floor. Eventually, when those in senior positions retired, there were many part-time midwives who had the ability, and qualifications which would have made them eligible for promotion, but the fact that they were part-time prevented them being considered. The result was that those much younger in the profession, and more importantly, often of little proven track record were promoted above those who had both. Some of these women were very able, others were not.

I became increasingly frustrated by this. I needed to influence the politics and policies of my profession which had to be left to others. I tried to keep these feelings subjugated and learned well the mantra that women could not have everything in life and that I was lucky to have home, family and career and for many years this had to be enough. Had I just been there for the money I would have simply got on with the job and left promotion to others.

## Problems for my employers

Having a subordinate who is able, aware and challenging is not comfortable and I know that though I was respected I was often viewed quite rightly as a thorn in the side. I asked questions about many things, which subordinates were not encouraged to do, and I had strongly held opinions on many professional issues. The wool could not easily be pulled over my eyes. I had been round the block too many times. This was no-one's fault it was just how the system worked. Many other women must have felt as trapped as I did. Personally, I had a very good relationship with my employers and, off the record, they often asked for my professional advice and opinion, and even more surprising they usually took it. I gradually learned to accept that this was how things must be. But today, with over 50% of the workforce now part-time, creative ways must be found to harness their abilities to a career structure, not only to fulfil their potential but also to meet the needs of the profession.

## Personal experience

Aged fifty, my children grown, my obligation to my parents happily discharged, and encouraged by my husband who has always believed that children and marriage had prevented my reaching my professional potential, I was now free to take on a new professional challenge. However, fifty in the workplace is ancient and really I had missed the boat. It is customary now-a-days to study for a degree to further a career. This is not what I wanted to do, by the time I had a degree what opportunities would there be for someone approaching their mid-fifties? Nor did I want simply to increase my working hours as physically running round a busy labour ward, working even more shifts and unsociable hours, was not appealing. However, I did want to do something for my profession which remained a passion.

I decided that my forthright opinions which for many years had been expressed in my workplace with limited influence, might be better elsewhere, where they may have more effect. With this in mind I decided to seek election to the Royal College of Midwives (RCM). RCM is the largest and oldest midwifery organisation in the world and concerns itself with the professional and employment needs of the UKs midwives. Much to my delight I was elected to Council, joining midwives from all over the UK to debate, discuss and give direction to midwifery. I relished the informed debate, became far more politically astute, and far less parochial. It was the beginning of one of the most exhilarating chapters of my life and I consider it to be the best professional move I have ever made. This was my time, those years between fifty and retirement. All the frustration and disappointment I felt as a result of lack of career advancement vanished. My election to Council, where I had the opportunity to influence things, I valued all the more because it had been a long time coming.

Totally unexpectedly, and as the result of a chance remark by a member of Council, I stood for election as President of the RCM in 1996 and to my great delight was elected for a 4-year term of office, after which I was re-elected unopposed for another 4 years.

The presidential role is an ambassadorial one, and doing it, I represent the country's midwives at home and abroad. To say it is the most wonderful position is an understatement. As well as fulfilling all my professional needs, it allows me to indulge two of my passions, eating and talking for midwives! I have discussed, debated and dined with royalty, members of both governments, colleagues from associated professions, such as doctors, nurses and health visitors, as well as midwives from throughout the world. It would be very difficult not to be inspired by it all.

**Conclusion**

In the year 2000's New Year's Honours List I was awarded a DBE and became Dame of the Most Excellent Order of the British Empire for services to Midwifery – I was absolutely astonished, and have barely stopped levitating with joy since. Of course it was the presidential role which caught the eye of the Prime Minister, but I like to think that the work I did for 30 years, directly looking after pregnant women, which represents the work most midwives do, was that which was really being honoured. I also like to believe that if a still part-time clinical midwife from Toxteth can find herself in such a wonderful position, anyone can.

Women, today, who for many years may have had to put their own needs to one side whilst juggling responsibilities, need to believe that their day will come.

It would be presumptuous of me to advise others how to organise their working lives, whether working full- or part-time. Women are good at finding their tailor-made solutions. However, my experience of many modern women is that they ask too much of themselves, risk becoming exhausted in the attempt, and have absolutely no time for themselves. Perhaps the reader would like to consider this quote, which though I still struggle with, I wish I had found earlier in my life *'Give commitments sparingly and honour them completely.'*

*A Personal View*

## Rosie Barnes

I had my first job at 15 – a Saturday job as a shampoo girl in a local hairdresser. I earned about 7s 6d (old money – we are talking about 1961) with the odd extra sixpence tip from kindly elderly customers. I learnt what hard work was and I learnt how not to be 'put upon'. My friend who was doing the same thing arrived very early, as requested, on the Saturday before Christmas and worked until 9.00 or 10.00 p.m. When she arrived home, exhausted, with not a penny more than the usual 7s 6d, her mother was so incensed, she insisted she went straight back to demand overtime payment. More in fear of her militant mother, I suspect, back she went, and got her extra payment.

It has always been one of my principles that 'if you don't ask, you don't get'. I'm neither a greedy nor a militant person, but I will not be exploited. However, in that frantic rush of getting the ladies of Radford, a poor area of Nottingham, suitably 'glamoured' – a local expression – for Christmas, the salon owner may not have given a thought to his long-suffering shampoo girl. The pitiful payment for her endeavours may have simply been an oversight. It could of course have been a blatant exploitation. However, the principle proved effective. My friend did ask and she did get.

Subsequent Saturday jobs in Pork Farms – a local chain of pork butchers – was followed by holiday jobs with them, soon to be followed by my first big breakthrough. My large extended family was a 'Player's' family. My Dad and several of his brothers and sisters worked at John Player & Son, the tobacco manufacturers. Indeed, my Dad met my Mum when as a 13-year-old, she was sent to work on his cigarette machine. His first memory of her was that she was too small to reach the machine and he had to fetch her a box to stand on. One of my maiden aunts, who had what they certainly thought was a far more prestigious job in the Player's offices, 'spoke for me'. In those days, some 40 years ago, paternalism on the part of employers was common. In Nottingham, whole families were often linked to a particular company, Player's, Raleigh (bicycles) and Boots being amongst the major local industries. So when I was 'spoken for' and subsequently offered a holiday job in the No. 3 factory canteen, it was regarded by all, including me, as an honour. The work was hard, physically tiring and the hours long. A normal day was 8.00 a.m. to 6.00 p.m., but it was paid for on a proper basis. The overtime rate was $1^{1}/_{2}$ times the hourly rate for evenings and double time at the weekend. In spite of paternalism, which didn't seem strange or unacceptable to me prior to my university days and the challenging of existing order that came later on in the sixties, Players was, in many ways a progressive company. Women received equal pay to men, the only difference I recall being our cigarette allowance. Men were given fifty cigarettes a week and women twenty.

This inequality never bothered me much, as after a few ineffectual and spluttering attempts with Perfectos, the Player's brand of my choice, I gave up all attempts to become an accomplished smoker. Rather than increasing my sophistication as I had imagined, the watering eyes and choking coughs identified me as a hopeless novice, a fate worse than death for teenagers who are required to appear experienced and nonchalant in every new adolescent situation. So, before we knew it was bad for us, and in spite of a strong desire to appear worldly wise, I did learn to listen to my body. Stiletto heels were in vogue for a while during my formative years, and I have given them up with rather greater reluctance. Being on the small, plump side, high heels seemed to me a far better alternative to cutting back on food and drink. They have had to go, though. To do a long day and to remain focused, you have to be comfortable in your body, so fashion has to be kept in perspective.

Player's and its attitude to women had changed considerably by the time I was old enough to work there. My Mum worked there until she was married, but then, as was the custom and the rules, she was obliged to leave. Player's, like many other employers, did not employ married women. The situation changed with the advent of the war in 1939. The men were called up, and as a protected industry keeping the troops in cigarettes, Player's couldn't meet its commitments without opening their doors to married women. Married women could stay on, but were required to leave when the first child came along, unlike Raleigh who did employ women with children. One of my aunts who took a job at Raleigh after her daughter was born was somewhat frowned upon for reneging on her maternal duty.

I learnt a lot in that canteen, returning during school holidays over several years. We produced drinks, snacks and dinners for several thousand people three times a day, served them, cleared up after them and kept the place clean – and clean it was. The food was simple, wholesome and cheap. If I remember correctly, soup and a roll cost $1^1/_2$d. This is all beginning to make me sound somewhat geriatric, but I'll press on! The other thing I remember vividly is the huge number of black people I served, many of whom had fierce tribal markings, as recent immigrants. As a little girl, I only knew white people. It must have been the wave of immigration in the late 1950s and early 1960s that changed the profile of Nottingham people, and the strangeness of these faces made an impression on me. Living in a multi-ethnic, multi-cultural society now seems so normal and desirable, but then, it was a very new experience.

One last point from this era. When I was 15 or 16 years old, I started my summer holiday job on the same day as another girl of my own age, who had left school and was starting permanent employment. We got on well and adjusted together to the other employees, the long hours and the nature of the work. We were two of a kind – carefree youngsters with everything to look forward to. When I returned the following year, I got a shock. She had aged and thickened considerably, and had acquired the world-weary resignation of some of the older women who had been there for decades. The difference between us was pointed. I got to know the older women quite well. They remain rich characters in my life, but the tedium of this kind of work for a lifetime was not for me. I knew I wanted something different and was determined to get it, even though what 'it' was eluded me somewhat.

One tip I was given in my early twenties and which I bore in mind has proved to be a mixed blessing. I was advised never to learn to type, as in the late 1960s, women at work were often sidelined to a secretarial or administrative role. If I wanted a managerial role, I had to be focused, not reduced to typing for male colleagues. Like so many things, it strikes incredulity in the younger generation that such a phenomenon existed so relatively recently, but I can assure you it did. So, learn to type I did not, which probably stood me in good stead for the next twenty years but has been a considerable disadvantage over the last fifteen years or so, what with the advent of the computer. So I will learn!

Since leaving university, I have had five entirely different careers, as a qualitative market researcher, a marketing executive, a primary school teacher, a Member of Parliament, and more recently Chief Executive of the Cystic Fibrosis Trust. I have enjoyed them all and feel privileged to have had such a varied and stimulating working life. So what tips would I give to my daughter for example?

Firstly, always be yourself. No-one can be happy if they are not true to themselves and very few of us can keep up a persona that is not really our own.

Secondly, be hard working and enthusiastic. A few of us get to the top easily and with a minimum of effort by luck or because of amazing talent, but most of us have to graft for it.

Thirdly, be positive. It is easy to write lengthy documents explaining why things can't be or weren't done, and to criticise everyone else's good ideas whilst never having one of your own but then no progress is ever made.

Fourthly, don't be afraid of failure. Take risks, albeit calculated ones. Nothing ventured, nothing gained. No-one thought I had a hope of winning the by-election in Greenwich, becoming an MP in 1987, including initially the electorate. But win I did, and handsomely at that.

Finally, be a person who makes things happen. That's what you're paid for!

## Linda Conlon

I was genuinely flattered to be asked to write a contribution to *Tips for Women at Work*. The publisher wrote to me stating he thought I was a successful woman who had achieved great things and that I might want to share some of the lessons I had learnt with other women. Who wouldn't be flattered?

I think he (not she!) might have revised his opinion if he had seen me in action a few weeks later having failed miserably to meet the deadline he had given me for submission of copy. So many things had crowded in on me. A last minute invitation to travel to Beijing to lecture on science communication involving much research, endless to-ing and fro-ing between Newcastle and China and conscious efforts to push the SARS alert to the back of my mind. Our own Science Festival – a first for Newcastle – that required not only a great deal of management time but also the reading of several thick, recently published tomes before interviewing the authors on stage in front of an audience. A major event attracting probably the greatest concentration of scientific talent the North East has ever seen, including two Nobel Prize winners. My daughter being admitted to hospital twice in two weeks, in great pain and no one knowing quite what was wrong with her. The peculiar smell from the downstairs loo seeping richly through the house as if a whole team of rugby players had used the facilities after a vindaloo curry. Oh yes, and my son ringing up in the early hours from university to discuss endlessly why the love of his young life had ditched him. Is it any wonder I had forgotten what a wonderful working woman I really was?

As I write this, I am conscious that my own list is one that could be replicated by working women – and working mothers – throughout the country. It's a juggling act that requires keeping so many balls up in the air at any one time that I can only sympathise wholeheartedly with Cherie Blair when she admitted recently to dropping one and making a clanger. Nor am I entirely surprised that recent statistics reveal so-called high flyers are not prepared to sacrifice their careers by stepping off the ladder and having babies – it costs a lot, it's exhausting and they feel that they never quite get back on the right rung of that all important ladder.

Male support in the home is incredibly important. Some women don't have it. I'm lucky enough to have fantastic support at home. But, however hard he tries, my husband is not a mother. He is not hard-wired to feel like a mother and when the chips are down, it's mum that the kids want. I cannot help but smile when I look at a postcard sent to me by a friend showing Fred Astaire and Ginger Rogers dancing divinely. The caption reads: 'Ginger Rogers did everything Fred Astaire did, but she did it backwards and in high heels'. Alison Pearson, the author whose recently published and highly successful novel, *I Don't Know How She Does It* (2002), charts the frantic life of working mother Kate Reddy, believes that '...sacrifice is written in our genes. It's part of the guilt chromosome we inherit from our mothers'.

Even as we move forward into the twenty-first century, I do believe that women have to be, if not twice as good as men, then at least much better than men to get as far as their male contemporaries. Of course it's not fair. The playing field is levelling out but it's still bumpy in places. There wouldn't be a need to publish a book called *Tips for Women at Work* if all was equal, would there?

Like most women, I suspect that I've not followed a life plan. They are fine for those single-minded, totally focussed women who cherish a burning desire to fulfil an ambition. I have nothing but admiration for them when they achieve their dreams. But I subscribe to the school that believes life plans are a bit like corsets – they seem like a good idea but in the end they just constrict you.

This is borne out by the fact that I have been a bit of a jack of all trades during my working life, ricocheting between jobs and disciplines – and finally ending up doing something I both enjoy and believe in. I've dabbled in marketing and public relations as an employee and as a freelance operator; urban regeneration and property development; and science communication and running a small business. I firmly believe that you can do just about anything if you have the passion and commitment to make things happen.

It is not easy to offer generic tips to working women. This book does that superbly well and I hope women will use it as a reference guide. Women are very different and what works for some women might not work for others. But from my own experience I would offer the following three guiding principles that I hope will strike a chord with all women.

## Try to do something you enjoy and believe in

We spend long periods engaged in work. It's a miserable, demoralising and exhausting experience to do something you don't enjoy or fundamentally just don't believe in. I hated my first job. It was sales driven, male dominated and just not me. From the minute I arrived, I spent all my time plotting an exit. I moved to a job that I enjoyed and to a culture I felt more at home with. Don't be afraid to recognise when you have made a mistake. Move on and do something you want to do.

### Don't be afraid to stretch yourself

However much we enjoy a job, it's easy to become cosy and opt for the safe and well-trodden path. We all need a challenge and a change if we are develop. Have a go at doing something that interests you but at the same time scares you! I spent almost 10 years as Director of Corporate Affairs at an urban development agency. It was a fascinating and high profile job but after so long I felt I could do it in my sleep. The opportunity arose to do something completely different – steering a millennium project through from concept to delivery. The two jobs could not have been more different. I was simultaneously terrified and elated! When the project was finally delivered, the sense of achievement I felt was overwhelming.

Earlier in my career, I applied for a job that stated applicants must be graduates with journalistic experience and should hold a clean driving licence. I was neither a graduate or a journalist – I couldn't even drive a car having failed my driving test 2 days before I sent in the application. However, I thought it was worth a go. Luckily for me, the field was a lean one. I was offered the job on condition that I passed my driving test within 6 months or they would ask me to leave. I passed and stayed in the job for five very happy years.

### Admit what you don't know

This is something women are much better at than men! We find it relatively easy to admit what we don't know and we know when to seek advice. Generally, men see it as a sign of weakness to admit ignorance. They feel they are losing face in a testosterone-charged boardroom. I have found that this ability to admit what we don't know is a very powerful tool in the female weaponry. While managing a huge team of architects, quantity surveyors, engineers, designers, lighting specialists – almost all men – I found the process so much easier to handle when I admitted that I did not understand all the technical detail. They were quick to explain, offer support and, together, we delivered a multi-million pound project on time and within budget – I had never managed anything remotely like it in the past. It's also very useful to be able to ask 'dumb' questions – it's amazing how many people sat round the table want to ask the same questions!

From my experience as both an employer and an employee it's worth acknowledging that you have children. Don't pretend that they don't exist! As an employee, I remember the time that I sloped off to attend my son's sports day. I said that I was going to a meeting but instead I took part in the mother's 100 metres sprint. I came a credible second and got a rosette for my efforts. I proudly displayed it on my chest and returned to work. My boss asked how the meeting went. Very well, I responded. I didn't realise you got rosettes for being at meetings, he said. Being a kind and considerate soul, he gently pointed out that if I'd needed time to go to a sports day event, I only needed to say so. Since becoming an employer, I've tried to emphasise to working mothers on my staff that nativity plays, sports days and birthdays are as important as anything in our business calendar. I've found that if I approve time off openly and up front for these events, then staff will repay this consideration many times over when I really need them to be around to fulfil business commitments.

Finally, I don't pretend to have identified the ingredients that make a successful working woman. There isn't such a magic formula. But I do believe that this book focuses on many of the common issues that we all face. It highlights and offers practical solutions and is an immensely useful reference book. Well worth dipping into when the going gets rough!

# Chapter 11
*Conclusion*

**Anna M. Maslin**

*Tips for Women at Work* has aimed to cover a range of topics that many of us find challenging as women in the workplace. *Tips for Women at Work* has given us the opportunity to reflect on key aspects of achieving success in the workplace. It has enabled us to consider important issues around the practicalities of the way we work including psychological preparation, CVs, interviews, salary negotiation, individual performance review, personal presentation, time management, childcare, stress, bullies and work-life balance.

How we spend our time is a useful indicator of where our priorities lie. Achieving seniority and a salary to match may be the dream of some young women but dreams also have a price. Is the price too high – have you negotiated the cost?

People friendly working policies for men and women are important for maintaining the fabric of community and family life. It is vital that women are aware of what is possible and what is reasonable so that they can benefit from the advances in policy and technology in the twenty-first century. Flexibility at one time was undervalued. Now many employers are able to recognise the value a flexible employee adds to the organisation and business objectives. Flexibility and new ways of working can help to ensure clarity of vision and the ability to approach work with a refreshed mind and body.

For professional success to be worthwhile for many women there is the need to adapt career patterns to accommodate family life. At present it is becoming more acceptable for women to continue to produce high quality work but using more people friendly work patterns.

Victoria Harrison summed up in *Women at Work* (2002):

*'I am pleased to have reached my current destination, but I cannot say that I arrived in it as a result of particular ambitions or sustained or coherent planning; it was more a matter of taking opportunities as they presented themselves. I believe that it is important to be flexible, to be prepared to change tack, and sometimes to do something completely different – particularly if trying to co-ordinate two careers in a family. I love my work, but I have never regarded the pursuit of any particular career as overriding. I hope that in future it might be made easier for women (and for men) to achieve a better balance, and to pursue interesting careers without the current macho pressures to work exceptionally long hours to the exclusion of other interests and family life.'*

*Tips for Women at Work* has tried to share principles, advice and tips to ensure women gain confidence when dealing with the world of work, whether at interview, appointment or in the workplace. It is hard to work out whether high levels of self-confidence precede the ability to succeed or whether it results from the success. The ability to turn a problem into an opportunity is a major contributor to a person's perception of their success in a given situation.

In *Women at Work* there was little doubt that for the majority of the women education was seen as central to their success. Although in *Tips for Women at Work* we have not focused on education directly that is not because we do not value it highly it is simply that in *Tips for Women at Work* we are offering a practical resource for colleagues in the here and now.

Dame Cicely Saunders advice in *Women at Work* was simple:

*'If I could pass on one piece of advice to other women it would be educate your children, especially the girls.'*

As editor of this book I would agree.

*Women at Work* endorsed the view that for an individual to be successful at work it does involve some planning for most people. *Tips for Women at Work* hopefully provided readers with some of those important tools.

It would seem that to be successful, in the round, you have to take a conscious decision where to concentrate your efforts based on your own priorities. Unlike some other studies in *Women at Work* we did find that the majority of women in our cohort did opt for a career and family life. For our group of highly successful women family life appeared to enhance their enjoyment of any success they achieved.

Rabbi Julia Neuberger stated quite simply:

> 'My greatest achievement has been to have two children, apparently reasonably well adjusted, who as adults seem to like spending time with their parents, despite our busy and chaotic life styles. As a professional, I think my greatest achievements have lain in moving on to the next thing without – I hope – leaving the people I worked with before feeling I had simply abandoned them. Family is hugely important to me. I have been married to the same man, Anthony, for the last 26 years, and we have a close family relationship, close also to our two mothers and my three brothers-in-law and their wives, and we live near the two mothers who were both widowed three years ago. I have a strong sense of family – and a strong sense of familial duty as well as pleasure.'

In *Women at Work* and *Tips for Women at Work* we have looked at work-life balance. There was a view, which came through *Women at Work*, that successful women with balanced work and professional lives tend not to over socialise.

Sarah Doukas from Storm, the highly successful model agency was quoted as saying:

> 'Most of my closest friends date back to my childhood and I've made an effort to keep these friendships intact. My early relationships are important as they keep me level-headed. I don't really socialise within the business and this gives me a more balanced outlook about the business and prevents me from being obsessive about it.'

Wheway and Ross-MacDonald (1998) recounted a story:

> 'There once was an famous American:
> He failed in business in '31.
> He ran as state legislator and lost in '32.
> He tried business again in '33 and failed again.
> His sweetheart died in '35.
> He had a nervous breakdown in '36.
> He ran for state elector in '40 after he regained his health.
> He was defeated for congress in '43,
> defeated for congress again in '48,
> defeated when he ran for the Senate in '55,

*and defeated for the vice presidency of the US in '56.
He ran for the Senate again in '58 and lost.
This man never quit. He kept on trying 'til the last.
In 1869, this man, Abraham Lincoln, was elected
President of the United States."*

I love this story. Is the moral to try, try, and try again or whether in fact you could be trying too hard. Abraham Lincoln was assassinated after he achieved his dream. It could be, as I said in *Women at Work* that sometimes we are trying too hard.

We all have hopes, aspirations and dreams. We all need to consider how our lives will have meaning in an uncertain world. Women are amazing. They can achieve great things, they can multi-task and they are often under-valued. I hope *Tips for Women at Work* will have given readers some practical resources in helping them achieve their goal and attain a healthy work-life balance.

## References

Maslin, A.M. (Ed.) (2002) *Women at Work: perspectives and experiences* (Newcastle, Northumbria University).

Wheway, T. & Ross-MacDonald, J. (1998) *The Sanctuary for the Mind* (London, Thorsons).

# Contributors' Profiles

### Sarah Doukas

*Founder and Managing Director, Storm Model Management*

Sarah oversees thirty staff at Storm's Chelsea offices. Her team includes fifteen model bookers and IT, PR and Accounts departments. Sarah herself continues to act as a booker; marketing, promoting and developing the careers of her models directly with influential fashion and advertising clients around the world. These include photographers, designers, fashion editors, casting agents, art directors and commercial directors.

Storm has been trading for over 16 years and currently represents over 500 models. Sarah feels it is her responsibility to represent her clients in a professional and ethical way. Sometimes she is their business manager or careers and financial adviser, and at other times she is just a friend and a good listener.

Her most famous discovery is Kate Moss, whom she spotted at JFK Airport in New York in 1988. Kate was fourteen at the time, and Sarah has been her model agent ever since. Storm has expanded over the years to include a Theatrical Agency – Storm Artists' Management, and two further model agencies in South Africa, one in Johannesburg and one in Cape Town. Today, models on the books include Kate Moss, Elle Macpherson, Sophie Dahl, Liberty Ross, Eva Herzigova, Jade Jagger, Dannii Minogue and Carla Bruni.

## Anna M. Maslin

*International Officer for Nursing & Midwifery*

Anna has had an outstanding career in Cancer Care working for many years nationally and internationally. She made a significant contribution to the development of psychological care for women with breast cancer. She also worked tirelessly on enhancing access to treatment information for women, particularly in relation to treatment decisions.

Her current work involves working with UN, government and non-governmental bodies on international healthcare developments. She has taken forward substantial pieces of work in Sub-Saharan Africa, India, South East Asia, the Caribbean and the Middle East. She has led work on HIV/AIDS, Human Resources for Health, Leadership and Healthcare Reform to name but a few.

Anna is very much a family person, married to Stephen for 22 years! She has four children, two teenagers, a toddler and new baby.


## Tom Storrow

*Director of Consulting with ATM Consulting Group*

Tom is Director of Consulting with the ATM Consulting Group, based in Staffordshire. He leads many of the ATM's major NHS-orientated assignments, including Trust mergers, the design and agreement of service strategies and performance and organisational reviews of hospitals, health organisations and clinical services. In addition, because of his personal interest and experience in the field, he delivers many smaller, customised coaching, personal and career development assignments. Led by Tom, ATM has just been appointed as a provider of Executive Coaching for the Centre for Health Leadership, Wales. He also regularly supports ATM's Search and Selection Division in their top-level recruitment work in the NHS and other public services.

Prior to joining ATM in 1997, Tom was, for 20 years, a senior manager in the NHS, the last five of these years being spent as Chief Executive of a General Hospitals Trust in the Midlands.

He has written for NHS journals and delivered many regional and national conference papers. He has had spells as a University Governor, a Trustee of a national charity and an Honorary Senior Fellow at Birmingham University's Health Services Management Centre. He continues in his long-standing role as a visiting tutor with the Leadership Trust in Herefordshire.

Tom's interest in coaching and development extends into his hobbies – he is an ECB-qualified cricket coach and helps to run his village club's junior section, where both of his sons' are keen players.

## Jennifer Parr

*Acting Assistant Director of Nursing*

Originally from New Zealand, Jennifer was educated as a nurse there prior to immigrating to the UK in 1991. She worked in a variety of surgical specialist clinical areas before undertaking and completing her midwifery education in Berkshire.

Jennifer designed, developed and implemented the inaugural International Recruitment campaign in New Zealand for orthopaedic nurses and midwives in early 1997 for the Royal Berkshire and Battle Hospitals NHS Trust. She then experienced International Recruitment from the perspective of a commercial recruitment agency for 18 months, gaining experience providing temporary and permanent placements to the NHS in London.

Jennifer took up the role of 'Nursing Officer for International Recruitment' at the Hammersmith Hospitals NHS Trust in 1998. She developed streamlined processes to support the ongoing strategy to recruit over 200 nurses each year to over 64 different specialities as part of the wider Recruitment and Retention strategy. She designed and implemented the first supervised practice policy and programme in the Trust and was fortunate to be involved in the NHS delegation to visit China in 2000. Jennifer represented the Healthcare Sector on the Work Permit User Panel of Work Permits (UK).

She was seconded to the Department of Health for 2 years and worked in partnership with colleagues in the NHS to establish an infrastructure in London to support increased collaboration, and quality processes supporting International Recruitment. She led on recruitment from the Philippines establishing a government agreement and developing a robust process to increase consistency and the ability of the NHS in London to recruit collaboratively. Jennifer contributed to the Guidance for the Provision of the Supervised Practice for Nurses and Adaptation for Midwives in London which was launched in September 2001. She has recently completed a Diploma in Systems Practice and BSc (Hons) from the Open University and returned to Hammersmith Hospitals NHS Trust where she is currently Assistant Director of Nursing for Practice Development and Return to Practice (Acting).

## April Brown

*Assistant Director for the NHS's Patient Safety Agency*

April qualified as a Registered General Nurse in 1992 at the QEII Hospital in Hertfordshire. She gained her clinical experience on medical wards at the QEII and Chase Farm Hospitals NHS Trust in Enfield, Middlesex. In 1997, April became a senior sister at the Luton & Dunstable Hospitals NHS Trust in Bedfordshire. The following year, she graduated from the University of Hertfordshire with a BSc in Health Studies.

Since 1999, her work roles have focused on workforce development and international recruitment and co-operation either at hospital level or within the NHS Executive for London and latterly at the Department of Health. This work has taken April world-wide and consequently her passport now looks rather impressive.

April has recently been appointed as Assistant Director for the NHS's Patient Safety Agency and she's also undertaking an MPhil PhD at the University of Hertfordshire.

What does this woman do to relax? April likes to run half-marathons, and is hoping to do the London Marathon in 2004. She also enjoys shopping for clothes and cosmetics. In addition, April is also a wife and a mother to a 5-year-old daughter.

## Andrée le May

*Reader, University of Southampton*

Andrée le May is Reader in the School of Nursing and Midwifery at the University of Southampton and Visiting Professor at Canterbury Christchurch College. She has a long-standing interest in factors that influence the quality of care that older people receive from health and social services and the evidence upon which practitioners base their decisions.

She has written and researched widely on these issues. Before moving into the Higher Education sector, she held a variety of community nursing posts and worked as a Research and Development Specialist Nurse. Her current research interests focus on the use of knowledge, by 'older' consumers of care and health and social care practitioners, in order to shape service change and delivery.

She has three children and lives in the south of England.


## Sue Harrop

*Planning Officer and Manager of Newcastle Early Years Development and Childcare Partnership*

Sue Harrop has been the Planning Officer and Manager of Newcastle Early Years Development and Childcare Partnership for nearly 4 years. Prior to this, Sue worked in Childcare and Community work, and taught Childcare and Early Years workers for 11 years. With three children, Sue has 22 years experience of juggling the demands of a job with the joys and challenges of family life.


## Sue Miller

*Senior Lecturer at Northumbria University*

Sue Miller is a senior lecturer who writes and researches into parenting education. She has been a teacher, a senior education psychologist and a Children's Services Manager. Her most enduring roles (and the ones she's enjoyed most) have been as a parent, as a writer on parenting support and as an advocate for the adoption of multidisciplinary perspectives in work with children and families. She has close links with the Parenting Education and Support Forum and speaks regularly at conferences and seminars on her work for agencies involved with parenting such as Health Action Zones and Youth Offending Teams. Currently she runs Care and Education at Northumbria University, is Chair of the Early Years Development and Childcare Partnership in Newcastle and is a member of the Associate Parliamentary group for parenting. She is probably best known in this context for publishing in the field of parenting education and for developing the parenting education materials; *Positive Parenting* and *Let's Talk Parenting*, both of which have been used extensively both in the UK and abroad.

## Catherine Gaskell

*Joint Mental Health Head for Prison Health*

Catherine was born and lived in New Zealand until 1985 where she completed her nurse training. She left New Zealand to travel through Australia, America and Europe and recommenced her nursing career in London in 1987.

She has worked as a clinician in a number of mental health milieus, including adolescent services, adult inpatients, day hospitals and a national Mother & Baby Unit. She has developed a strong interest in women's health and issues around parenting.

Catherine's career to date culminated in an Executive Nurse Directorship for a Community Trust moving to another Directorship in a large specialist mental health trust in London in 2000.

In 2003, she undertook a secondment to the Department of Health to assist in developing enhanced mental health care within prisons as the mental health lead, which is a national post but based in London.

Her life requirements for the chapter *Dealing with the Unexpected, Stress and Bullies* are as a nurse working in the NHS. Catherine is in one of the top four recipient bullying groups, according to the UK National Workplace Bullying Advice Line.

As a senior manager, Catherine has witnessed bullying behaviours displayed by other senior managers and has used colleague's actual experiences to illustrate the chapter.

As a women who works outside the home, wife and mother of two sons, living with an au-pair and a mad dog, Catherine can personally vouch for the stress-busting tips!

## Heather Angel

*Freelance wildlife photographer, author and lecturer*

Heather is perhaps best known as a highly versatile wildlife photographer whose pictures have a strong artistic appeal as well as scientific authenticity. After a zoology degree, she took up photography whilst undertaking research in marine biology. When her first book – *Nature Photography: Its Art and Techniques* – was published in 1972, Heather's photographic career took precedence. She has produced 47 titles on photographic techniques, natural history and gardening topics.

For more than a quarter of a century she has been at the forefront of wildlife and nature photography in Britain and her work has been recognised by many awards both here and abroad. On the publication of her acclaimed book *Natural Visions*, *Practical Photography* described her as 'the doyenne of nature photography'.

Heather was President of the Royal Photographic Society from 1984–86 and Nottingham University made her a Special Professor in 1994, where she teaches part of the MSc course on Biological Imaging. Her major exhibition *Natural Visions* has been touring Britain since June 2000 and a replica exhibition was on view in Kuala Lumpur, Cairo and Beijing in 2002–2003.

Heather's son, Giles, is a seasoned traveller, having accompanied her on many overseas trips as a child; now he collaborates with Heather and has recently designed her website www.naturalvisions.co.uk.

## Dame Lorna Muirhead DBE

*President, Royal College of Midwives and practising midwife*

Lorna is the President of the Royal College of Midwives, the oldest and largest midwifery organisation in the world. She is also a practising midwife. She has worked as a clinician predominantly on a labour ward in a teaching hospital, which does in excess of 6,000 deliveries a year. Lorna has had a long and distinguished career. She lectures frequently and maintains a passionate interest in promoting clinical standards. Her most recent published work was as a member of the working party on the joint Royal College of Midwives/Royal College of Gynaecologists document '*Towards Safer Childbirth*'.

## Rosie Barnes

*Chief Executive of the Cystic Fibrosis Trust*

Rosie Barnes has three children. She has worked continuously since leaving university in 1967. She has had five quite different jobs over these years.

The first years were spent largely in qualitative market research, currently known as 'focus' groups, followed by 5 years as the Social Democrat Party (SDP) Member of Parliament (MP) for Greenwich. Having lost her parliamentary seat in 1992, she then moved into the charity sector and is currently employed as the Chief Executive of the Cystic Fibrosis Trust.

## Linda Conlon

*Director, The Life Science Centre, International Centre for Life, Newcastle upon Tyne*

Linda Conlon has been the Director of The Life Science Centre for the past 8 years. Prior to this, Linda was the Director of Public Affairs, Tyne and Wear Development Corporation.

Linda's impressive CV contains many achievements including being invited to advise the Polish and Greek governments on the feasibility of establishing science centres in their respective countries, the preparation of the detailed proposal for The Centre for Life Science Village Project that won £27 million from the Millennium Commission and presenting the successful bid for sponsorship funding from the Wellcome Trust.

Linda is married with two children and lives in Newcastle upon Tyne. Away from her busy schedule Linda enjoys travel, reading and walking.